Denim

+

Visible Mending for Beginners

2-in-1 Mending Bundle for Denim, Knitted Fabrics, and Other Materials

Table of Contents

Book 1: Denim Mending for Beginners

Book 2: Visible Mending for Beginners

Denim Mending for Beginners

Patch and Repair Your Favorite Denim with Classic Japanese Stitching

Jikoshoukai: The Introduction

People have been sewing for a very long time.

20,000 years ago, during the Ice Age, someone decided that punching a hole through needles and running threads through them seemed like a good way to sew.

They were right.

Archeologists have uncovered needles made of bone and concluded that early humans used them to sew furs and skins. But bone needles required, well, bones. There had to be a better material to utilize.

Fast forward to the year circa 100 B.C. Parts of Northern Europe began to use iron needles. These were sturdier than any previous forms of needles used (bronze was used to make needles around 3,000 B.C., and these had been in use until iron replaced them).

Today, you have sewing needles made from materials such as carbon steel (for that extra durability) and 18K gold (for corrosion resistance and for those who do not mind splurging a little on tools).

It is not just the tools of sewing that have evolved over the years. Even the reason behind the art of sewing has shifted perspective. At one point in time, it was a craft used for necessity. People could not afford to risk sacrificing animals they used as food to mend a torn shirt. These days, sewing has turned into a hobby. It has become a way for people to enjoy an art that requires a considerable amount of skill. It has even become a way to improve your mood and help you relax.

Even technology has helped add convenience and sophistication to the art. Thomas Saint is known as the designer of the first sewing machine. Although, a German by the name of Charles Weisenthal had issued a patent for a machine that used needle nearly 30 years before

Thomas Saint's design. Because of this reason, there has been some debate on the matter of the actual inventor of the sewing machine.

Regardless of the machine's origins, people and industries both use the machine today to create and repair garments, fabrics, clothing, and fashion products.

Companies use workshops that contain sewing machines to manufacture textiles, and those textiles are used to create clothing and apparel. In many cases, manufacturers produce the article of clothing themselves, especially if the manufacturer is a home-based business. From tops and trousers to dresses of all kinds, sewing comes into play in the creation of many clothing products, and in the mending of those products as well.

Need a solution to fix a tear? Why, sew the tear together. Is there a way to make some modifications to a garment? No problem, bring out the needle and thread.

This capability to sew damaged clothing allows clothes to last for a long time. It makes them reusable. It helps maintain them.

It makes them sustainable, even in the world of fashion.

Chapter 1 - Tsuru: The Tools

Tools of the Trade

Even though a sewing machine speeds up the mending process, hand sewing is often preferred. This is because sewing performed by hand allows you to take the time to create wonderful and high quality handcrafted results. In many cases, the results speak for themselves, as you get to see the work of a person who applied finesse and patience to create a spectacular finish.

This is what you will be producing: works of incredible quality that showcase your skills.

When people think about the tools that are required for sewing, they often imagine the needle, thread, and scissors. While those are definitely the essentials, each sewing process requires a different set of tools. Take, for example, the process of marking the cloth. You have markers to show you where the pleat should fall on the garment, where the dart should be inserted, and so much more. Looking through the different markers, you have so many options such as water-soluble ink pens, the ever popular tailor's chalk, the tracing wheel, and a lot more. Those are just for the markers.

You have tools for ripping seams. You have special tools for opening buttonholes.

For the work that we shall be doing, we will dispense with the tools that are clearly meant for veterans of the art. We are not working with seams and buttons, so we won't require any tools that attend to those parts.

What we have left are tools that are important for you. These are the basic tools that will help you perfect some of the techniques that we are going to focus on.

Before you can start working on your material, you need to organize your tools. It is always preferable to keep all essential tools near you so that you are prepared before you begin mending. One of the reasons for this is that while you are mending, you often lose yourself in the work. Sewing requires a fair degree of concentration, and you might not want to be distracted while you are engrossed in a particular stitch.

Here are the tools you may require:

- A sharp needle. Ensure that you are not using worn or damaged needles, as they might cause damage to the denim while stitching. For specific stitches or threads, make sure that you get the right needle. To highlight an example, sashiko thread goes perfectly with sashiko needles.

- Thread. The choice of thread is important because when you use a thread that does not match your requirements, it only creates a poor result. There are a lot of factors to consider such as elasticity of the thread, its seam strength, its chemical resistance, and more. So ideally, you should get a high-quality thread and the right one for specific stitches.

- Pins. For holding the cloth in pace. After all, you only have two hands.

- An iron to smooth out the fabric. This allows you to work on the denim more easily. Additionally, with an iron, you can remove any folds or creases that might hinder your work process.

When you are ready, let us dive in to the first stitch.

Chapter 2 - Sashiko: The Little Stabs

Sashiko is a form of classic Japanese embroidery that makes use of curved or straight linear patterns to form stitches. In other words, it uses curved or straight stitches made in a repeating pattern. The name itself means "little pierce" or "little stabs." The name is used to describe its technique, that of a running stitch that has numerous little stitches.

What makes Sashiko special is the fact that no one knows of the technique's exact origins. All they know is that it developed in rural areas in Northern Japan. From there, it spread along the trade routes to different parts of the world.

The spread of the technique occurred during the Edo period as early as 1615, which is why by the time the Meiji period arrived in 1868 the technique was already well established in various parts of Japan.

Sashiko stitches are usually sewn into fabrics and materials using a white thread on an indigo background or fabric. This was because most Japanese families were too poor to afford dyes and colorings. They utilized whatever materials they could get their hands on, and blue fabric was one of the most common materials available during that era.

Today, sashiko patterns are a beautiful addition to a wardrobe. They are versatile in that you can apply them on almost any piece of material. As they are hand-sewn, you can adapt the technique to fit different patterns for various articles of clothing.

We are going to utilize this technique to create stitches that are not only effective in mending your denim, but add a simple design that creates a wonderful effect. Whenever you are ready, let us find out just what materials you might require for the process.

Materials Required

You will need all the materials mentioned in Chapter 1. Do make sure that you are using sashiko needles and threads for this stitching. You will also require the below equipment:

- Scissors
- Fabric chalk for markings. **PRO TIP:** If you do not have fabric chalk, you can also make use of dry soap (wet soap is, of course, slippery and does not make for a fun sewing experience).
- Ruler
- The right fabric (discussed below)

The Right Fabric

Traditionally, people use Sashiko on dye-fabrics, particularly indigo dye. But that is not a rule set in stone. Any color of fabric will do, provided that the fabric is smooth and even.

PRO TIP: when choosing the size of the fabric, make sure that it not only covers the gap or hole you are about to mend, but extends beyond the hole's borders to cover a large area. In other words, choose a fabric that is almost the same size as the hole. However, in many cases, people have been known to use the exact measurements as the gap that they would like to stitch. This has its own advantages that we shall discuss further below. As you are getting started, we are going to give you enough surface area to work with.

For example, if the hole you are mending is 3 inches by 2 inches, then you should ideally choose a fabric that is 5 inches by 5 inches.

This allows you to have an extra area around the hole to extend your pattern. The amount of area you would like to work with depends on your preference. You can use a bigger fabric so that you can add a bigger pattern to your denim.

Pattern

For our stitch, we shall go ahead and use a classic sashiko pattern. This is a simple pattern that allows you to complete the work quickly and also acts as a primer to get you started on sashiko stitches. Mastering it is relatively easy and once you get used to it, you can move on to more complex patterns. The basic idea that we are going to employ is that you keep the stitches going until you complete the pattern.

Our first step is to use a chalk or any other form of marker to draw the lines on which we shall be performing the stitch. This applies not just for this instance, but to all stitches that you might work on in the future.

The pattern we will be using for this stich is a lined pattern. We will be working with multiple parallel lines. You will understand how to create the lines in the following section, but for now, it is important to know the basic idea of the stitch.

The number of lines you require depends on the

size of the gap on the fabric. Let us assume that you have a gap that is three inches wide. You are ideally looking to add around six to seven lines that run across the gap.

I would recommend adding the lines lengthwise along the denim. This makes the stitch easier to work with for beginners. However, you could work with diagonal lines (based on the position of the fabric).

Each line features a quarter of an inch stitch, followed by an equally long gap, then a quarter long stitch, a gap, and so on until you have mended the patch.

It is not necessary for each stitch to be parallel to the others, as long as the lines along which the stitches are made are parallel.

Getting to Work

Now that you have your pattern ready, it is time to perform the stitch.

Step 1:

The first thing that you should do is ensure that the gap or hole is devoid of any stray threads.

I use the term "stray threads" to talk about those threads that surround the hole and are usually uneven.

Take your scissors and cut off these threads.

You do not have to make each cut perfect. You are merely removing those strands of thread that are jutting out too much.

Step 2:

You are now going to use your chosen fabric to cover the area.

Place the fabric on the inner side of the denim. This is the side that comes into contact with your body, with the side that is visible being the outer side of the denim. Make sure the hole is covered properly.

When you are satisfied with the result, use your pins to secure the fabric.

Step 3:

Take out your fabric chalk (or your dry soap), and start making lines on the outer side of the denim. Use your ruler to make the lines straight.

PRO TIP: Once you have made your first line, take a step back to see if you have aligned the ruler properly for the next line. What you should also do is make sure that your lines match the area of the fabric placed below the hole.

There is no point in adding a line on a part of the denim that does not have fabric underneath. Additionally, your first line should start close to the edge of the fabric in order to allow for as many lines as possible.

The gap between each line can be either half an inch or a quarter of an inch. However, the smaller the gap between the lines, the more thread you might require to finish the job.

Step 4:

Take out your Sashiko needle and thread it with about 19 – 25 inches of sashiko thread. Try to keep the length between the aforementioned measurements or else you will have a thread that dangles a lot. This makes for an uncomfortable sewing experience.

Step 5:

Add a knot to one end of the thread. Choose the line that is closer to the edge of the patch. Now take your needle and insert it from the bottom of the patch (from the inner side of the denim).

Additionally, make sure that you are starting at the top or bottom of the line, and not somewhere in between.

What you are about to do is use a technique called "running stitch." In this technique, you will make sure that you are not going to pull the thread through after you have inserted the needle.

This means that the stitches you add to the fabric will be continuous as you move from one stitch to the other.

Step 6:

Now you are going to start creating the stitches. Each stitch should be around a quarter of an inch long.

Here is a great way to keep track of your stitches. Starting from the inner side, pierce the denim. Measure quarter inches, and then pierce again.

Then measure quarter inches again and pierce the denim again. Continue doing this. Make sure you do not pull the thread through or you will have a difficult time getting back on track.

When you reach the end of the line, ensure that

the needle is on the inner side of the denim before moving on to the other line.

When you reach the other line, pierce through the denim and bring back the needle to the outer side. Measure ¼ inches and pierce through and continue repeating the pattern you created on line one.

PRO TIP:

Do not worry if the stitches are not uniform. You are just starting out. The most important thing for you to do is enjoy the process. Immerse yourself into the technique and get into the flow of things. There is no need to be perfect. As you keep practicing the technique, you will gain mastery over it.

Uneven stitches are also designs of their own, in many ways. See if you can use that to your advantage and make a unique pattern out of it.

Step 7:

If you find yourself running out of thread, then make a knot on the inner side of the denim and tie it off.

PRO TIP: Anticipate the fact that you are running out of thread and make sure that you reach the end of a line before you create the knot, rather than having the thread run out in the middle of a line. It is much easier to start from the top or bottom of the line than from the middle.

Step 8:

Continue creating the stitches until you have covered all the lines you have made.

PRO TIP: Take a pause occasionally to smooth out the denim. This removes any unevenness and helps you create better stitches. You can use an iron if you like, but do not take too much time using the iron. Just a quick swipe to smooth out the denim should do.

Step 9:

When you have finished with the last line, create a knot (any simple knot will suffice) on the inner side and complete your stitch.

Step 10:

Admire your handiwork!

As you can see, by using a simple pattern, you have turned a piece of denim that had a flaw into a work of art. You are now the envy of your friends!

PRO TIP:

- There is a reason why we use sashiko thread for this process. The thread is thicker and most importantly, it is twisted in a unique way. Even if you have a thread that has the same thickness as sashiko, do not replace the sashiko thread with it.

- Some people have known to sharpen their needle before using it. This is not necessary. In fact, sharpening the needle might end up dulling it if done improperly. However, I do recommend that you know how to sharpen your needles so that when you do spot signs of dullness, you are prepared for it. In the beginning, what you should think of doing is getting yourself a high quality needle. Manufacturers already keep the needle sharp and ready for the sewing process.

- If you feel that the needle tends to apply pressure on your finger and leaves behind blisters, then you could avoid the discomfort by getting a thimble. A thimble is simply a small plastic or metal cap worn on your finger in order to protect it. You typically place it on the finger that you use to push the needle. Let us take an example. If you tend to push the needle using your middle finger, then go ahead and place your thimble on it. If you notice yourself pushing the needle with your forefinger, then that is where you need to place your thimble.

Chapter 3 - Kantha: The Patched Cloth

A famous method of marketing certain fabrics and cloth in India involves prefixing them with the word "Kantha." You will often find names such as "Kantha blankets," "Kantha fabrics," and so on. The word itself is a selling point because it denotes a type of craft that deals with precision and quality. The word "kantha" has two meanings:

- In one meaning, the word translates to "patched cloth." This meaning refers to kantha's ability to patch together various fabrics to create unique quilts.

- Another meaning refers to the type of stitch used on fabrics.

However, kantha mainly refers to the type of stitching that is commonly found in Bangladesh, or in the Indian state of West Bengal.

When you look through history, you can trace back this style of embroidery all the way back to the pre-Vedic ages. Like many forms of embroidery, kantha utilizes motifs to a greater degree. A majority of these motifs are representations of nature. They focus on elements such as the sun, the universe, and on many occasions, the tree of life. To people using the kantha stitching form, it was merely a way of life. They used it to sew together torn garments or fabrics. It wasn't a marketable skill, and they were definitely not focused on creating customers for it.

That soon changed. Kantha began to spread to various parts of the world. This spread occurred mainly because of the use of kantha in Hindu festivals, traditions, and occasions. From weddings to social occasions to religious events, kantha began to be viewed by more and more people. Soon, there were people who wanted to know more about it. They wanted to try out the stitchings themselves. They wanted to practice it.

Some of them wanted to create products made out of kantha stitches.

What makes this embroidery special is that for centuries, Indian women have been using old cloths or discarded materials and stitching them together using a running stitch. They have transformed materials that were old and useless into something beautiful and useful. In fact, the entire idea behind kantha was to create something to provide warmth and protection, which is why it resulted in the creation of exquisite blankets based on centuries of experience. Eventually, the method of stitching took on a life of its own. It shifted from merely stitching blankets to mending various fabrics and garments.

Materials Required

You will need all the materials mentioned in Chapter 1. For the kantha method, you do not need a specific type of needle. My only recommendation is that you use high-quality needles that are not bent or worn out. Apart from the materials mentioned in Chapter 1, do note the materials below:

- Scissors
- Fabric chalk for markings. If you do not have fabric chalk, you can also make use of dry soap.
- Ruler
- The right fabric (discussed below.)

Fabric for Kantha

When it comes to Kantha, you can work with any fabric. But as you are mending denim, I would recommend getting a similar denim fabric as the one used by your article of clothing.

PRO TIP: Should you feel like you want to, consider getting a fabric that is a shade lighter or a shade darker than your denim clothing. This makes for an interesting effect and allows you to add a sense of uniqueness into your clothing.

Additionally, having a darker shade can help you blend the fabric in with the denim fairly well. It won't entirely disappear, but it won't be noticeable, either.

Pattern

The best part about Kantha is that it incorporates numerous stitching techniques to create wonderful patterns. Not only do you get to work with different patterns, but you can also see the technique used for creating incredible patterns on items such as tote bags, belts, quilts, jackets, and other accessories. But we shall, of course, be working on denim, and to get you started on the technique, we are going to utilize one of its simple patterns.

This time, we are going to use a spiral pattern to

create our designs.

With the spiral design, you automatically get used to working with curves. This, when combined with the lines that we practiced with in the sashiko technique, will allow you to create spectacular ideas for your stitching patterns.

So let us get started.

The first step you have to take is to make sure that you have placed your fabric right. We are going to use the same method to place fabric as we did in the sashiko technique. We will place it on the inner side of the denim (the side that comes into contact with your body). Remember that the fabric should be larger than the hole (for now, until you are used to the stitching technique).

When the fabric is large, you will notice that when placing the fabric, you not only cover the hole, but you also ensure that you work with stitches around the hole.

When you have arranged the fabric underneath the hole, the next step is to draw the pattern. Here are a few tips that you can follow to make sure you get the pattern right.

- The starting point of your pattern should be near the edge of the fabric. However, you can choose any edge if you like. For example, if your fabric is shaped like a square, you now have four edges. Your spiral pattern can commence near any edge.

- Take your time when drawing the spiral. You need it to go inwards towards the center of your design.

- As you draw the spiral, you will start to notice that there are numerous concentric circles. The space between each circle should ideally be the same.

- However, you can intentionally create the spiral with a few flaws in its shape, just to give it a unique twist. Do make sure that none of the lines intersect each other.

Once you have completed the job, take a step back to examine the result. Make sure that you are satisfied with how the design looks.

If you think that you might have to change the shape, do it now before you begin stitching.

Because you will be working with a slightly more complicated stitching technique, you might require a little more practice to get it done perfectly. For this reason, take your time stitching the pattern. Enjoy the process itself.

If you feel that you have made a mistake, then you have nothing to worry about. That is what scissors are for. Simply snip away the threads that have gone, let's say "off-track," and continue on with your work.

When you are ready to continue, let us begin to stitch the design into the denim.

Getting to Work

Step 1:

Ideally, you should start at one end of the spiral. You could begin at the end that lies in the center of the spiral design or the one that lies near the edge of the fabric (as discussed above.)

I would ideally recommend stitching based on how you created the spiral. As you started drawing the spiral from the edge of the fabric and moved to the center, you could begin your stitch from that point and slowly move towards the center as well.

The main reason for this is that we will be stitching back in the opposite direction. So it is better to get used to going in one direction first.

Step 2:

As with the sashiko technique, choose anywhere from 19 inches to 25 inches of thread. If we require more, then we can knot off the thread the way we did in the Sashiko technique and then add more thread.

Step 3:

Start from the inner side and pierce through the fabric to bring the needle to the outer side. We will now begin to follow the rules of the running stitch method. Add a quarter of an inch stitch and then pierce through. Let there be a gap of about a quarter of an inch, and then create another quarter inch stitch. Continue doing this as you work your way around the spiral towards the center.

Step 4:

If you run out of thread, then you can create a knot on the inner side of the denim and tie it off. As we are not working with straight lines, it is not easy to guess exactly how much thread we might require before we reach the end.

Once you have created the knot, add a new thread. Measure about a quarter of an inch and then continue with your stitch. Begin on the inner side of the denim. Pierce through, measure a quarter of an inch, and then go back to creating your running stitch pattern.

Continue doing this as you move towards the center of the spiral.

Depending on the size of the spiral, you could be using multiple threads to get the job done. Once you reach the middle, make sure you end the stitch on the inner side of your denim. Use a knot to finish the first part of your stitch.

Once you are done, we can now move on to the

next phase of the stitch.

Step 5:

We will now be moving backwards along the spiral. For the first phase, you moved from the outer side of the spiral towards the center. This time, we are going to start at the center and back our way towards the starting point of our stitch.

What you are going to do now is cover up all the gaps that were created during your initial run of the stitch. As we are starting at the center of the spiral, find the final gap of your stitch (this should be the gap that is closest to the center of the spiral).

Step 6:

As always, we are going to start on the inner side of the denim. Pierce through and create your first stitch in such a way that it covers the gap.

Once the stitch is complete, your needle should be back on the inner side of the denim.

PRO TIP: If possible, do not cut off the thread after you had completed the first phase of the stitch. Without cutting, bring the thread back around to fill up the first gap. This creates a better result for you once you have completed the entire stitch.

Step 7:

Continue stitching all the way back to the starting point. If you run out of thread at any point, simply create a knot on the inner side of the denim and use a fresh thread to continue your stitch.

Eventually, you will have all the gaps stitched as well.

The result is that you now have a spiral that does not have a single gap in it. The best part about this technique is that if you look at the inner side of the denim, you will notice that there are no gaps there, either.

PRO TIP:

- After you have completed drawing the spiral design on the denim, you could place the thread on the design to find out approximately just how much thread you might require in the end for the stitch. When you have discovered the length of the thread, simply add another three or four inches to it. This extra length becomes useful when you have reached the end of the spiral and plan to continue backwards.

- If you do not mind working with a long thread, then simply use the above measurements and double the length of the thread you would like to use. This should give you enough thread to work your way towards one direction and then back again.

- Variety is spice, after all! So try choosing a color that compliments your denim's color. For example, if it is blue (which it typically is), then you could use tones that have low contrast like grey, purple, or even black. However, should you wish to add a dash of bright and warm colors, then choose to use high contrast shades such as red, orange, or yellow.

- The best way to work with colors is by

placing them against the denim. Try each color and examine it from afar. See how the color looks on your denim. More importantly, ensure that you are comfortable with the color combination. If you feel that none of the colors mentioned above work for you, then try out a different color of your choice and then check out the effect it has on your denim. Whatever shade you choose, let it add a bit of personality in your stitch and bring out an incredible finish.

- A way to keep track of whether you are doing the technique right or wrong is by looking at both sides of the denim. You should be able to notice the gap-stitch-gap pattern on both sides. After you have completed the kantha stitch, you should notice no gaps on either side of the denim.

Chapter 4 - Boro: The Repaired

Boro has gained somewhat of a reemergence in recent times because of the way in which manufacturers and brands can utilize it to create stylish and chic clothing. What makes boro unique is its ability to utilize different fabrics to get a desired result.

Unlike other forms of stitching, the rise of boro was due to a sense of necessity. Its use was accepted more to accommodate the mending of torn and damaged fabrics than to create any sense of aesthetic presentation.

This style of stitching was popular in the rural areas of Japan during the eighteenth and nineteenth century. This was because cotton was not introduced into Japanese culture until well into the twentieth century. When a particular piece of clothing or covering material began to show signs of gaps or thinning, the family who owned the materials would find any piece of fabric that they could find. They would utilize the technique of sashiko stitching to get the job done.

Since rural families could not afford to purchase new articles of clothing, they would continue to use the damaged garment for as long as possible, often handing them over to the next generation. These garments would continue to gain more patches as they suffered more holes and tears. Eventually, what was left was a garment that was devoid of its original design (or even colors).

When these fabrics that had received boro stitching were discovered during World War 2, it created a renewed interest in the method. What was once a technique utilized for living in moderate comfort soon became a fashion sense that spread to different parts of the world. However, to many Japanese, the boro fabrics were a remnant of a past that reminded them of their rural upbringings.

But as the adage goes, time does heal all wounds.

In modern day Japan, people have begun to adopt boro stitching as a way to work with fabrics. There are companies that especially work with the boro technique to create fashionable garments and accessories.

We are going to use this incredible technique to mend denim. We will see how boro stitching can create such a wonderful splash of color, fun, and style out of your torn garments.

Let us begin.

Materials Required

You will need all the materials mentioned in Chapter 1. For the boro method, it would be ideal to use the sashiko needle. You should also use sashiko thread to work with boro stitches. As always, I recommend using high-quality needles that are not bent or worn out. Apart from the materials mentioned in Chapter 1, do note the materials below:

- Scissors
- Fabric chalk for markings. If you do not have fabric chalk, you can also make use of dry soap.
- Ruler
- The right fabric (discussed below).

Fabric

When you are working with the boro technique, you have a choice between two fabric palettes:

- You can choose to stick to indigo dyes and find various shades of indigo, blues, and other similar hues.
- You can add in a dash of other complimentary neutral shades such as blacks, browns, and whites to bring a pop of color.

- One of the things that we are going to try is using different fabrics for the same patch. You could also use one single fabric to get the desired result. However, to add more personality to your denim, you could try multiple fabrics.

- A good way to decide if you are indeed looking for a single fabric or numerous colors to cover up the gap in your denim is to place your choice of cloth against the denim. Place them the way you would like the finished stitch to appear. Then see if you are satisfied with the result.

I would also recommend getting plainly woven, light fabrics that do not have tight stitches.

So whenever you are ready, let us move on to creating a pattern.

Pattern

We are going to be working with a running

stitch again. This is because boro uses the techniques of sashiko to complete the mend. However, this time, we are going to work along the borders of the fabric. So if your fabric should look like a piece of square or a rectangle, your stitches will have a square or rectangular finish.

The arrangement of the fabric depends on the number of fabrics you have chosen for the stitch. But regardless of how many materials you have chosen, we will still be working along the border. Confused? Don't worry. It will become clear as we work our way with the stitches.

Getting to Work

Step 1:

Place the fabric on the inner side of your denim the way you want to stitch it. If you are using multiple fabrics, place them beside each other. Make sure that a part of one fabric overlaps the other so that they can be stitched together.

Let us assume that you have three fabrics now; blue, black, and white. Place the blue fabric first. Then place the black fabric on beside it, but let a small part of it fall over the blue fabric. In a similar manner, use the white fabric in such a way that a part of its edges falls on the black fabric.

If you would like to avoid arranging the fabrics in the manner described above, then you have an alternative. Try the below technique.

Take out your trusty scissors and create strips of fabrics.

Now examine the hole that you would like to mend. If the gap is mostly a horizontal tear, then place your strips of fabric vertically to allow each of them to appear through the gap. In a similar manner, if the tear is mostly vertical, then place the strips horizontally. Ensure that the strips overlap each other slightly so that you will be able to stitch them together. The size of each strip depends on the size of the tear. Let us say that the tear is 5 inches wide and 2 inches tall. Each of your strips should be 2 inches wide and roughly four inches tall. This allows you to arrange the strips in a manner where each strip can be noticed and also ensures that the hole is covered properly. Once you are done, secure the fabrics with pins.

If you are using just a single fabric, then you don't have to worry about adjusting it. Taking the above example of a tear which is 5 inches wide and 2 inches tall, simply find yourself a bit of fabric that is 6 inches wide and 4 inches tall. With that, you are good to go.

Once you have your fabrics ready, make sure that you pin them together.

Step 2:

Now that you have put your fabric or fabrics together, it's time to create your markings. For each side of the arrangement, draw two parallel lines. This means that you should typically have four pairs of lines if your fabric is square or rectangularly shaped.

It does not matter if your lines end up intersecting each other. You can use the intersections to make your pattern look unique.

Step 3:

Next, take out your sashiko needle and thread it with your sashiko thread. If you like, you can use a comfortable thread length of 19 to 24 inches. However, you can also place the thread against your markings and then check for the exact length that you will require for the stitch.

You can now perform the stitch in two ways. You can start with one line and begin sewing it constantly until you reach back to where you started from, or you can start with one straight line, stitch it, and then knot it before moving on to another line. I personally prefer the first option, as it is smoother and takes less time.

Step 4:

As always, start from the inner side of the denim and then begin your stitches. Use the running stitch method and keep your stitches and gaps at a quarter of an inch.

Step 5:

Make sure that when you reach a corner, you move your stitch to the next side and continue stitching.

Remember this. Since you have a pair of lines, you will have the outer shape and the inner shape.

What does this mean?

Let us look at it with an example.

Let us say that your fabric is square shaped. The lines that you draw on your fabric will also be shaped as a square. Because you are going to use parallel lines, it will look like you have a square that contains another small square within it.

Which is why - when you start stitching – you should make sure that you are focusing on the outer shape first.

Only after you have completed stitching the outer shape should you move on to the inner shape.

Step 6:

Make sure that you have completely stitched the outer shape and created a knot. Once that is done, proceed to stitching the inner shape.

Step 7:

Once again, use the running stitch method to create the stitches for the inner shape. You might use a shorter thread length to complete this section since the shape itself is smaller.

Step 8:

You can stop any time in the process to iron out creases or folds. This will allow you to work with a smoother surface. Furthermore, uneven surfaces prevent you from making accurate measurements. The result is an awkward finish where you have certain stitches meeting the length criteria of a quarter of an inch and others looking longer.

Step 9:

When you are done, take a step back to admire your work.

PRO TIP:

- One of the things that you can do is practice the stitch on a sashiko kit. These incredible practice tools allow you to hone your craft before you can actually put them into practice.
    - These kits come with surfaces that have marked lines. Stitch along these marked lines until you are comfortable working those stitches on fabric.
- Muscle memory is a fantastic ability of the human body. It is why guitarists are able to perfect their skills and artists can draw their ideas without much effort. In the same way, the more practice you perform, the more your muscle memory improves.

    - Using the sashiko kits mentioned above, make sure that you try out different stitches. I would recommend starting with the running stitch, which you can use on practically any garment and for several purposes. Once you have perfected that, move on to other forms of stitches that provide a bit more challenge to you.

- You are only limited by your creativity. Seek out ways to add color to your garments wherever you see fit.

- If you find yourself unable to find fabrics, then you could use old clothes in your house. The best part about using old clothes is that you do not have to discard what remains. You can simply use it for another garment that requires stitching.

- Try to create your own designs and find ways to implement them. This process might allow you to flex your creativity and discover your own style for doing things.

- Here is an important point to remember: there is no such thing as a mistake in stitching. You are beginning your stitching journey and the most important factor is that you are having fun.

- If you find yourself in a situation where the thread might seem too thick, then you could try separating the strands to make a thinner thread.

- Your garment will be divided into two segments: the stitched areas and the stitch-free areas. Whenever you are adding stitches, think about how the stitch-free areas might look. This way, you can actually create interesting designs and patterns.

Chapter 5 - Patchi: The Patch

There are many ways one can use a patch.

Getting a hole or a tear in clothing is inevitable. But, there are many ways to repair the damage caused. This is where patches become important. All you have to do is pick out the damaged garment and then mend its tears by using a patch above it.

You could add a patch as an addition to your clothing, giving it a sense of style or adding a unique perspective to an old material.

Additionally, some clothing – like uniforms – come with patches on them or require patches. You could hand sew these patches.

Or, you could add a pocket to a shirt. The idea is the same. You simply have to sew the preferred patch into the shirt, right where you would like the pocket to be. However, the only difference this time is that you have to keep one side open (which, of course, is the top of the pocket).

In many ways, patches are fun to work with because you can create incredible designs with them. You can use a multitude of shapes and colors to come up with your own spectacular results.

We have already seen many ways to sew an underhand patch, which is a patch that lies underneath the garment or, as per the phrase used in this book, the inner side of the garment (the side that comes into contact with your skin).

Now, we shall take a look at how we can create an overhand patch. This patch falls outside the garment. In other words, you sew it into the face of the garment.

Before you begin to sew the patch, you must get your garment ready for the process. There are a couple of steps that you can follow to make this happen. Here is how you can make that happen:

Step 1:

Make sure that you wash and dry the item of clothing on which you would like to stitch a patch. This is especially true for new articles of clothing. If you patch them up and then decide to wash them, you might notice that the material underneath the fabric will bunch up. This would make it necessary to remove the patch and try to sew a new one in its place, which I am guessing you wouldn't want to do.

Additionally, if you are using cotton, the fabric tends to shrink after you wash it for the first time. If you stitch the fabric before you run your clothing through the wash, then the material under the patch might shrink, causing the patch to shrink and bunch up as well.

Step 2:

The next step that you should take is to iron your clothing before you apply a patch to it. This helps you to avoid working on creases, which not only give you an uneven surface to work with that puts your measurements off, but also bunches up your patch.

The most important point to remember is that you should ensure that you iron out the area where you are going to apply the patch properly. If you can do that, then you may not have to use the iron again when you are adding your patch.

Choosing the Fabric

If you take a look at the market, there is no shortage of fabrics that you can use for your patchwork. However, one of the most important questions that one has to ask is what kind of fabric should one use?

You might think that simply picking an option that has the right color might just suit your purposes. However, that is far from the truth.

So which fabric should you use? Well, there are a few options that you can work with. I recommend using natural fabrics that have a tight weave. Let us take a look at some of the natural fabrics in the market such as cotton, wool, linen, and silk. Not only do they have the right weave, but they are also the best fabrics to use for hand sewing. Their surfaces are strong and you can easily create decorative stitching on them. One of the best features of the aforementioned natural fabrics is that you can pass your needles through them smoothly. This is because they include fibers that are woven in a cross pattern, creating minute gaps for you to use.

Let us now explore each of the above fabrics and understand why they are ideal for sewing. Once we cover their properties, I will let you know which fabric works the best for denim.

Cotton

Probably the most commonly used fabric is cotton. However, you might find quite a few varieties of cotton on the market. The trick is to pick out the right one. Thankfully, you have yours truly to guide you. You should be looking to get yourself a quilting cotton. The main reason for this choice is that quilting cotton is made to fit sewing and embroidery purposes. Plus, it is easily available on the market because of its use.

Linen

This material is lighter than cotton, but it is also slightly stronger. Linen is made using raw materials from the flax plant, and many even consider it as the strongest form of natural fibers. You can use this material to add a bit of durability to your finish. Linen is also a good conductor of heat. This means that it can sap away the body heat from you easily, keeping you much cooler than other fabrics.

Silk

Here is a common misconception about silk; people often think that the material can tear easily. But the reality is far different. In fact, it is a well-known fabric because of its tensile strength, which allows it to withstand strong pulls. Another feature of silk that makes it preferred my many embroiderers is the fact that it is also slightly elastic. This makes silk easy to work with and provides ease-of-use when sewing. Furthermore, silk does not wrinkle easily, retaining its original shape as much as possible.

Wool

Wool is a rather resilient fabric. It can not only handle heat well, but it is not affected by mold and mildew (two forms of fungus). Wool also prevents allergies by keeping dust mites away from your skin. In fact, dust mites do not like wool at all! The fabric can also keep you cool during summer. In short, wool is a strong and incredible fabric to work with for patches.

Fabric Mistakes

One of the most common mistakes that people make when choosing a fabric is that they look at the aesthetics and the colors more than the material itself. It can be easy to fall prey to this situation. After all, when you look at a fabric that has a certain appeal, you obviously imagine the many ways in which you can use that fabric.

What you should be doing instead is finding the right fabric for the project you are working on. Let us take a look at denim. You would never try to add silk to the material, as they do not go well together. However, silk does provide an assortment of colors that you can work with, making it a rather tempting fabric to you.

The best fabric that you can use for denim is regular cotton. You can choose to use quilted cotton as well, but using regular cotton is easier since you more than likely have materials at home that you can use.

Now that you have an idea of the fabric to use, here is how you can add a patch to your denim.

Step 1:

Get a high quality needle and thread. You should ideally use a sashiko needle and thread it with sashiko fiber. When choosing the thread, make sure that it is either the color of the denim or it matches the color of the external patch. If the patch has multiple colors, then you should match the thread to the color at the border of the patch.

If you cannot find a thread that has a similar color as the patch or the denim, then you could choose a close darker shade.

You could also choose a lighter thread, but that depends on the results you expect. Do you want the thread to be easily noticeable, or would you like to blend it into the fabric as much as possible?

Step 2:

Position the patch in the way you prefer.

PRO TIP: Try out different angles and positions to find out what suits you best. You might have an idea of how to place the patch, but it does not hurt to experiment a little. Who knows? You might just discover a better alternative.

Step 3:

Use pins to secure the patch in place. If you like, you could also try out the denim and see how the patch looks on you. Of course, you have to be careful of the pins. Don't poke yourself for a simple trial!

Step 4:

Using a chalk or a dry soap, start adding lines to the fabric. The lines should resemble the same shape as the fabric, as close to its edges as possible. If possible, keep the line uninterrupted and continue drawing until you reach back to the point you started from.

Step 5:

Take out your needle and as usual, poke the patch from the inner side of the denim. If your patch has corners, then it is better to start at one of the corners. However, if your patch is circular or does not have a corner, then you can start anywhere you like.

Step 6:

Use the lines to guide your stitches. For the patch, we shall go ahead and use a regular running stitch that we are now pretty good at using. You can use the quarter inch rule here as well with the stitches and the gaps.

Step 7:

If you run out of thread, simply use the techniques I had recommended in the previous chapters. However, for this purpose, I would simply recommend you measure 25 inches on the thread and begin using it for the stitch. Typically, most patches would not require you to use more than 25 inches. However, should you find yourself running out of thread, simply knot at a specific point and get the spool of thread to add more to the needle. Continue from where you left off by measure a quarter inch gap. Piece the material from the inner side of the material at the quarter inch mark.

Step 8:

Work your way around the fabric until you reach back to the beginning of your stitch. At this point, you could start threading in the opposite direction. This will allow you to close off the gaps that were originally there. This is not necessary and is entirely up to the result you are trying to achieve in your sewing. If you would like to find out how to close gaps, look at the chapter for Kantha to know more. When you reach the end, knot your thread.

Step 9:

Using your scissors, cut off any loose threads that you notice.

PRO TIP:

You know by now that you can get cotton from any old material or clothing. One of the ways to get fabric out of a material is by first measuring the area on which you would like to place the patch. Then, trace that area on another material. Cut out the fabric that meets your measurements and use that to sew it into your denim.

You can use multiple colors as well. For adding different colors, do refer to the boro tutorial mentioned above. It will give you a few ways in which you can use different colored fabrics.

Once you have finished your work, make sure you iron the fabric again. I would also recommend frequently ironing when you work to keep the fabric straight.

You can use the above technique to not only repair denim, but also add a bit of color and style. Try out different colors and shades until you find the one that is suitable for you. After that, it is just a matter of following the above instructions.

Chapter 6 - Yoeki: The Solution

When you are working with stitches, you often come across many questions that leave you befuddled. Each person's experience with sewing is unique. Some grasp concepts easily, but others take a while to master the process. This is in no way a reflection of the skills and abilities of the individual. Rather, it is how the individual prefers to learn.

I believe that everyone learns in their own way and at their own pace. This might be the case with you. Do not be deterred by the fact that others have learnt a skill quicker. The most important thing for you to remember is that you should revel in the learning process.

There is no competition. So take your time to master the techniques.

But in order to answer some of the questions that beginners might have, I have created a handy FAQ section right here. While the section does not involve a comprehensive list of questions, I based this on some of the most common questions I get asked about sewing.

Should you put the patch inside or outside the hole?

There are many reasons that can justify both options. Whether you would like to sew on the inside or on the outside entirely depends on what you aim to achieve and the type of patch you are working with.

Let us examine the result you would like to see on the denim.

If you plan to stitch a patch on the inside, then you get a subtle look. Something that is not outwardly presentable but still adds a sense of diversity to your denim. In other words, you can make your denim look stylish without having to display the style on the outside.

When you add a patch on the outside, then you are showing a bold look. You are showing off a bit of your personality in a very visible manner.

That being said, one of the main reasons that people should consider whether or not they should use a stitch on the inside or the outside is by examining the type of patch that they are working with.

If you are using a patch that has no designs and simply has a plain color, then you could place the patch on the inside of the denim. This serves two purposes.

- Placing a patch on the inside looks more aesthetically presentable than using the patch on the outside. You can, of course, experiment with different colors to find the one that fits your needs. But ideally, you should use the patch on the inside. Plus, revealing the tear while showing a material underneath it is quite a stylish addition.

- It is much more convenient to work from the inside. This is because you are typically piercing the patch from the inside. You can keep the outside for making markings for you to follow when sewing.

Again, it is also based on your decision. If you prefer to block the tear entirely, then you can choose to keep the patch on the outside.

On the other hand, if you have a patch that has some sort of print, text, image, or other design, then you should ideally use the patch on the outside. This is to ensure that the graphic is not blocked from view. In some cases, the graphic could be small enough for people to see through the tear in the denim. In such cases, you could use the patch on the inside with the graphic or pattern showing out.

There is no rule set in stone when you are working with patches. What you create is entirely up to you. As I had mentioned before, try and have fun with your creations and experiment with different styles. The best way to find out if the patch goes on the inside or on the outside is for you to test it out against the denim. If you are comfortable with the patch on the inside, then that is what you should choose. If you find out that the patch is meant to be outside, then you have your answer!

Should you make the patch bigger than the hole?

The simple answer to this question is yes. You should ideally look to make the patch bigger than the hole. This becomes important when you are working on the patch from the inside. You do not want to run out of patch when you are using a particular method of sewing. Additionally, you might decide to create a complex pattern on your denim. You might want the pattern to be seen clearly. With a larger patch on the inside, you have a bigger canvas for your sewing art!

Another factor to consider is that with a bigger patch, you can attach it to the denim more firmly. You can add more stitches and cross-stitches. to ensure that you have the fabric sewn properly into the denim.

On the other hand, if you are working on the patch from the outside, then you could use a patch that is almost the same size as the hole. This makes for an interesting effect. With the number of options available to you, you can experiment with the fabric to see what fits your needs.

I had provided this recommendation for the previous question, and it holds true for this one as well; try out the patch against the denim to see how it looks. If you are satisfied with the presentation, you can make up your mind after that.

Should you make extra stitches around the repair area?

When you are working with tears, gaps, and holes, one of the questions that you might find yourself frequently asking is whether or not you should add in extra stitches to your patch. For the previous question, I had mentioned how, by using an extra area of fabric, you can ensure that you sew the fabric properly into the denim.

But is that the only reason for considering whether or not you would like to add extra stitches?

The entire act of creating stitches is an art in itself. You are using a simple – or complex – design and basically using it on your clothes (in this case, your denim). With that process alone, you are adding more designs and style to your denim than it had before. Would you like to show more of your stitches? Do you want to try adding different and more unique stitches around the repair area? Do you have a particular design in mind for the stitches that might require extra space?

By using just the running stitch technique, you can create many unique patterns on your denim. Some of these patterns do not require a lot of space, and you can sew them into the fabric you are using. Others might require more space, depending on the complexity and the number of lines you would like to use for the pattern.

Think about what you are going to sew and how you would like to accomplish it. Once you have figured out a rough idea for your stitches, you can choose how much area you would like to use.

Another thing to note at this point is that you do not have to use extra space immediately. What I mean by this is that you might first use fewer lines, avoiding the use of extra stitches. If you change your mind later, you can always come back to your work and add more lines, depending on the pattern.

How to reinforce the inner thigh of your jeans?

Rips in the thighs of jeans are a potential threat to anyone who has thighs.

That's everyone.

However, some people experience this issue more than others.

The best way to deal with this problem is to reinforce your jeans from the inside. It is quite tempting simply to discard your jeans for a pair of new ones. You could always buy yourself new jeans. After all, a rip on the knee or almost anywhere else on the jeans does not look so bad, but one on your inner thigh might just be slightly embarrassing.

Thankfully, there is a simple way to reinforce your jeans so that you can prevent such rips and tears from occurring.

Before we start, we have to get the jeans ready for sewing. Let us start with that.

Step 1:

Make sure you wash the jeans before you sew them. Ideally, you should turn the jeans inside out and let them have a proper wash.

Step 2:

Once they are dry, iron them while still keeping them inside out to remove any folds or creases on the jeans.

You are now ready to stitch on your jeans.

Make sure you have all your materials ready. You will need the materials mentioned in Chapter 1 for the most part. For the patch, you do not have to worry about choosing a specific color. If you can find other, similar jeans in your home, then cut out a small patch from those jeans. Regarding the measurements of the patch, I would recommend getting one that is 5 inches by 5 inches.

PRO TIP: If you would like to strengthen the reinforcement, then you can take two patches, both of which are 5 inches by 5 inches, and place them together.

If you would like to see how the size fits on your jeans, then simply take a chalk, measure 5 inches by 5 inches, and draw the shape on your jeans. See if the size is ideal for you. If you prefer a bigger size, then draw that shape on your jeans and check if it satisfies your preference.

Once you have confirmed the size, you can then go about getting the patch from another pair of jeans. If you do not have jeans, you can also use cotton from any piece of clothing you have in your house (preferably one no one is using)!

Now you are ready to start stitching the patch into the inner thigh.

Step 1:

Now that your pants are inside out, you need to place an object (preferably a small book or a box) on the other side of the surface on which you are going to perform the stitching. This is to ensure that when you use your pins, you do not accidentally pin the legs of your jeans shut.

Step 2:

Since you are only reinforcing your jeans, find a thread color that has a darker shade than the jeans. This will help you hide it well. The best kind of thread is one that matches the color of the jeans. Such a thread would completely blend into the jeans.

Step 3:

Now place your patch where you would like it to be. Use pins to secure the patch to the jeans.

PRO TIP:

If you like, you can use the tip above where you can draw the outline of the patch on your jeans to see exactly where you would like the patch to be. Once you have the outline, you can place your patch on it.

Step 4:

Thread your needle. You can use the sashiko needle and thread for this stitching, or you could use any other needle and thread, the choice is yours.

Since the pattern of your stitching won't be visible to anyone, you do not need to draw lines to create a stitch pattern. However, you can use it to make sure you are stitching in a particular direction and don't suddenly find yourself stitching outside the patch area.

Step 5:

As always, run your needle from the inner side of the jeans. This means that you will pierce from the side that is facing you. Typically, I would say that you should start piercing from the inner side, by which the needle would pierce out. This time, the needle will pierce in. The reason we are doing this is because once we complete the stitch, we will be tying the knot on the inside of the jeans, which is the side you are currently looking at. If the jeans were the right side out, then you would be piercing from the inside.

Step 6:

Use a running stitch method and continue stitching all the way around until you reach back to the starting point.

Step 7:

Upon reaching the starting point, create a knot to secure the patch to the jeans. The knot should be visible to you (unlike the previous cases where the knot was on the other side of the material). When you turn the jeans around, you will notice that the knot itself is not visible.

Step 8:

Now you are ready to wear your jeans. If you would like to perform the same technique on the inner thigh of the other leg, then you simply have to follow the same steps mentioned here.

You have now successfully reinforced your jeans!

10 Jean Repair Hacks

I have been placing some pro tips for you all throughout this book. However, I thought I would compile all the important hacks that I think you will find useful into one spot. Here are 10 jean repair hacks that you should know about.

- The first hack I would give you is more of advice; always fix the holes in your jeans rather than throwing them away.

- If you feel like your zipper is damaged beyond repair, then all you need to do is use a keyring to create a loop around your zipper and your jeans button.

- To add a splash of color, find a fabric or fabrics with floral prints and then sew them to your jeans.

- You do not have to stick to one layer for any repair; you can use up to three layers!

- Do not buy separate denim cutoffs – you can make them in your home using just your scissors.

- If you have a piece of gum stuck to your jeans, simply place a cube of ice on it for a while, and then remove it easily!

- When your jeans are loose at the waist, simply use an elastic band on the back of the jeans (where you find the loops) and stitch it to the pants.

- If your jeans button falls off, then stitch a piece of fabric behind the buttonhole and run the button and the snap through the fabric.

- To keep your jeans from shrinking in the wash, wash them using cold water, heat them for about ten minutes, and then air dry them if they are still damp.

- If you find your jeans decoloring, then simply place the jeans in a solution of water and vinegar for a while before sending them to the wash!

Leave A Review?

Throughout the process of writing this book, I have tried to put down as much value and knowledge for the reader as possible. Some things I knew and practice, some others I spent time to research. I hope you found this book to be of benefit to you!

If you liked the book, would you consider leaving a **quick review** for it? It would really help my book, and I would be grateful to you for letting other people know that you like it.

Ketsuron: The Conclusion

Fashion is a constantly evolving culture. It produces new designs, ideas, and products year after year. And every time a new statement is made, new clothing and apparels become the trend. However, fashion is also an industry that is capable of causing wastage in the form of discarded textiles and other materials.

To avoid such wastage and help make the industry sustainable, we can turn to the very source that creates the clothing and apparel: sewing. Using techniques like "minimal seam construction," which reduces the number of seams sewn into clothing, fashion can save materials and reduce waste. By reducing waste, fashion can contribute towards sustainability and help protect the environment.

But sewing does not just help the fashion industry. It helps people, too.

I have known people who claim that sewing is

therapeutic. In fact, it is not just the people I know, but a majority of the public that has begun to work with the sewing craft. One of the things that you might hear quite often is that the process has been shown to have some remarkable effects on managing stress.

Mental effects notwithstanding, everyone has a different reason for working with hand sewing. Some have chosen to hone their skills so that they may eventually start a business out of it. Some prefer to use sewing as a form of a hobby. Still others aim to satiate their curiosity.

Whatever your reasons for entering the sewing world are, remember that like all other forms of art, it requires practice to become a master. But with sewing, the satisfaction, enjoyment, and fulfillment do not lie in the fact that you are eventually going to be really good at the craft. Rather, it lies in the very act of practicing hand sewing.

My biggest advice would be this: take your time

with each technique. When you have gained a fair amount of confidence with a technique, then try a different pattern and see how well you do. The whole idea behind sewing is to use your creativity to come up with interesting designs. After all, there are those who have stitched even things like animal patterns into fabrics!

You could also use numerous sewing practice kits that are specifically made for you to try out patterns, techniques, and even different types of tools.

With that, I hope you enjoy hand sewing.

Tanoshinde!

Visible Mending for Beginners

How to Mend Knitted Fabrics and Other Materials With an Artistic Touch

Introduction

Mending is the sewing of a cloth or clothing that is pierced or torn. Do you, too, have torn clothes that you would like to sew? If so, you will find what you are looking for in this book. While it is easy to find videos and visual guides on how to mend, there are not many written manuals about visible mending.

In this book, I will go over different mending methods and explain what you can do and how you can do it in detail. You will find lists of necessary equipment, steps to be followed to mend in different styles, and solutions to hide the mending. You will also learn about stitching distressed jeans, repairing socks, hemming jeans, and many more things.

The following chapters are all about versatile ways to mend different fabrics. It is true that a sewing machine is one of the most important investments in a seamstress's life. But when you are a beginner or you just want to learn how to stitch things by hand, a sewing machine is not necessary. This book will help you discover some alternatives to start slowly discovering the world of sewing before investing in a sewing machine.

The first thing you can do is start learning to sew by hand. Even if you own a sewing machine, sewing by hand remains relatively frequent since using a machine is not very practical when it comes to small things. Learning to sew by hand will be very useful for future projects and you can better understand how sewing works!

You will also learn about different, more traditional ways of stitching. A wrong choice of fabric can be disastrous when it comes to mending. This is a common mistake among beginners and can be hard to fix, but fortunately, it can be easily avoided with good preparation. With each section, you will have a list of things you need and tips and tricks that will help you achieve your best work.

When you sew by hand, you make stitches like those made by the sewing machine. There is a wide variety. These stitches are intended for particular purposes. For example, some serve to assemble two pieces of fabric, to finish a garment, or to make a specific piece. The chosen point also varies depending on the type of fabric with which you are working.

Sewing by hand seems simple. However, like any manual work, hand sewing requires a method. By following it, you have all the chances to succeed in what you undertake. I present you some general tips about sewing by hand and if you respect them, your work will be easier.

For sewing lovers who want to learn the basics, the following chapters are some techniques to learn basic ways to sew by hand. Through different projects, you will acquire more experience in sewing.

Chapter 1: Stitches

Before sewing, you must know how to thread a needle correctly. This may seem easy, since it is only a question of passing the thread in the eye of the needle. However, there are some precautions to take to avoid tangling the thread. Its length is very important. If it is too long, the thread may get tangled and you have to thread your needle again. Normally, you should cut a piece of thread about 50 cm long. If you do not have a measuring tape near you, this length is about the same as your arm, from shoulder to wrist. Once you have the right length, you cut the thread. Use a pair of scissors to cut, and don't rip/break the thread, because it will not slip through the needle well afterwards.

You hold the needle by putting the eye in front of a light to clearly distinguish the opening through which you pass the thread.

After the thread is through, you make a knot at the end. If your vision is weak, you can use a needle threader. This is an instrument that makes it easier to pass the thread through the eye. First, you insert the opening of the needle threader into the eye of the needle. Then, you pass the thread through the opening of the needle threader and pull the threader back through the eye. This will thread your needle.

Before you start sewing stitches, you need to knot one end of the thread. Then, prick the needle into the fabric by pushing it from the back of the fabric toward the spot you want to stitch. To finish the stitching, make a knot in the shape of 8: make a small stitch, pass the thread inside the loop and pull. Do these two or three times to secure everything. The thread should not come undone if the knot is done correctly.

Things you will need:

- A needle, depending on the fabric you want to mend. For sewing, the needle must be fine if the fabric is fine. You will find the type of needle needed next to the fabric options to be mended below.

- Variety of threads (solid) depending on the type of the fabric. When you buy a spool of thread, it is generally indicated which fabric the thread is suitable for. If you have doubts, you can choose a thread suitable for all fabrics. In general, the color of the thread is chosen so that it is as close as possible to that of the fabric.

- A thimble, if you have one. The thimble is placed on the middle finger and is used to push the needle through the fabric, avoiding pain at the end of the finger.

- An embroidery hoop to help you stretch out the fabric.

Satin Stitch

A satin stitch is used a lot in embroidery and can be used to cover imperfections. It looks like a solid, shimmery piece of fabric once it is completed. It is composed of very tight threads, in stitches of 3 to 13 cm in length. The stitches are close together, forming a solid image. When done correctly, the stitch will be illuminated by light and look absolutely stunning. Sewing a satin stitch by hand requires a certain level of precision. At first, practice on unused fabric. This way, you will have some experience, a good idea of the position of the points, and learn to sew them as tightly as possible without ruining your good fabric.

The Technique

- Use your embroidery hoop and tighten some fabric between the hoops. By doing this, the fabric will remain tense and flat during your work. Before you get into the complex patterns of satin stitch, start with trying to stitch a regular square or circle.

- Tie a knot at the end of your thread to stop it from escaping the fabric.

- Push the needle in from the bottom side

of the fabric, where you want your shape to begin.

- Embed satin stitches as tightly as possible and do not exceed 1.25 cm in width. The satin stitches that are too long will float with space between the fabric and it will cause disorder.

- Tighten the points as much as possible. There must be no empty space between two points.

- Sew stitches as tight as possible without intermingling the threads, in parallel and narrow rows. Do this as slowly as possible to make sure you don't have to start over. Pay close attention to your work.

- Make sure the threads are evenly stretched with every new stitch.

Tips

Practice satin stitching until you get enough

tight threads to lie flat, but loose enough not to deform the fabric. Sewing the points too tight is a classic mistake. Try to stretch the dots evenly or your threads will be too loose.

Make a satin stitch in your test fabric. Once you feel confident with your experience, move on to a real project.

Here are some ideas:

- Embroider the edge of a garment.
- Design the monogram of a project.
- Sew a buttonhole with a very narrow satin stitch.

When you feel ready, tackle a piece of art designed exclusively with satin stitches, and remember that all satin stitches must be tight.

The Best Fabrics for Satin Stitch

- **Aida fabric:** Commonly available in craft stores and absolutely perfect for beginners. It is 100% cotton and usually comes with a large variety of threads.

- **Fiddler's cloth:** A mix of polyester linen and cotton. It is very easy to stitch on and comes in different sizes.
- **Klostern:** A mix of rayon and cotton, easy to stitch on and fun to use.
- **Cotton:** A classic you can easily find anywhere. You are more likely to find items of cotton fabric around your home to practice your satin stitch.
- **Silk:** Can be hard to work with for a beginner but once you feel confident in your silk stitch, you will love working with silk fabric. It looks sophisticated and gorgeous with some silk stitching.

Duplicate Stitch

Duplicate stitch is also called Swiss darning. It allows you to go over your knitted project with stitches of a different color to add more dimension to it. When a duplicate stitch is done carefully, you should not be able to tell that the stitches are not knitted, without a close examination. This is a wonderful way of adding some color to your knitting projects without having the need to learn complicated knitting techniques.

The Technique

- Decide what shape you want, where you want to do your duplicate stitch, and how big you want it to be.

- Insert the needle on the bottom side, one line under where you want your design to start.

- It is better to start creating your desired stitch from the right side of the design.

- The trick is to follow the natural shape of the knitted fabric to make it look like your stitches are knitted- hence the name "duplicate stitch".

- Follow the line of the natural shape of the knit and find two legs you can push the needle through.
- When you push the needle through the two legs, you should have your first stitch that duplicates the fabric.
- Follow the natural shape of the knitted fabric back to the first spot you inserted your needle.
- When you complete two stitches, pass the needle through the back of the stitches vertically.
- Continue your desired shape by moving towards the left.
- Always remember to follow the shape of the knit and finish by inserting the needle back where you started.

Here are some ideas:

- Make a flower on your knitted scarf.

- Add a heart on the outer side of your wool gloves.
- Duplicate stitch your initials on your beanie.

Remember!

Only use the same kind of thread you used for the knitted project while creating a duplicate stitch to make it look realistic.

Invisible Stitch

When sewing by hand, it is important to know the technique of the invisible stitch. This stitch will allow you to make liners or join two pieces of fabric without the thread being visible.

The sewing machine is our best friend in sewing, let's face it. But learning to sew by hand can sometimes also be very useful. In this section, you will learn how to sew an invisible stitch by hand. If you are a beginner and want to practice this stitch, you can sew your own washable cleaning wipes as a start.

If you are about to finish a cushion or other padded creation and you need to close it, nothing is simpler or more discreet than the invisible stitch.

Necessary tools for this stitch:

- A thimble

The Technique

- Get a thin needle.

- Take the needle and pass some sewing thread of the same color as your fabric through the needle eye.

- Choose a thread of the same color as your fabric. Even though this stitch is, as its name indicates, "invisible," it is better to be smart and to remain uniform.

- Iron the two edges to be connected by marking a clean fold. With this trick, the work will be easier and smoother.

- Immobilize the fabrics you want to sew with some pins. Keep the pins close to the area you want to stitch but not directly on the area.
- Make your first stitch by passing the needle under one of the fabrics, where the fold is. This will hide the knot.
- Then go to the opposite side and slide the needle through the second fabric horizontally.
- Go back to the first fabric and slide the needle horizontally to pick up the fabric.
- Go back and forth on one side and then the other.
- Use the straight stitch technique and do not hesitate to hold the two edges firmly between your fingers, thus avoiding irregular points.
- Pull the thread as you go along to shut the fabrics together.

- From your first stitch, your goal is to make long stitches on one side of the piece of fabric and short stitches on the other side.

- You must now be very careful when entering and removing the needle from the fabric to create the seam to make the thread invisible or almost invisible.

- When you get to the end, pick up some more fabric from inside the fold like before and create a thread loop. Push your needle through the loop twice to secure the thread.

- To hide the thread, pierce the needle through the fold and bring it out from inside the fabric. Bunch up the fabric to shorten the thread and cut the thread. This will hide the end of your thread perfectly.

Tips

- This technique is also called the mattress

point or the hidden point.

- Use the thread of the color of the piece of fabric that will be most exposed to sight. This way, your seam will be much less visible.

- If you use thin, long needles, your aim will be better, and the holes will be smaller.

- Pay attention to your fingers and take the necessary precautions when sewing like using a thimble.

Here are some ideas:

- Use this technique when hemming pants, skirts or other clothing items.

- Use it to finish blankets or pillowcases.

- Use it whenever you desire a perfect finish where the thread won't be visible.

Cross Stitch

Very different from traditional embroidery techniques, and much easier, the technique of cross-stitch embroidery is performed by a succession of small crosses that are embroidered on top of each other to form a pattern. Often, you will hear "counted stitches" instead of cross stitch. Indeed, to achieve embroidery, it is necessary to count the number of small crosses to form the pattern. You know how to count, so you'll know how to embroider!

Necessary tools:

- Embroidery cloth
- A needle
- Embroidery thread
- A pair of embroidery scissors
- A cross stitch pattern (printed out, cut out, etc.)

There is a canvas made especially for cross

stitch embroidery. Beginners always start by embroidering on an Aida canvas. It is ideal to begin with because it is woven with small holes that show the place where you will insert your needle.

The Technique

- Tie a knot at the end of the thread and take your needle from the bottom side of the fabric, on the same line as the start of your embroidery.

- Bring the needle to the front of the canvas on the starting point of your first cross-stitch.

- Start embroidering through the knot, making sure to cross over the thread on the back with each stitch to secure it.

- Hold the tail of the thread against the back of the fabric in the direction that you will embroider and work the first 4 to 5 points on this thread each time.

- Make sure the dots cover the thread on the back of the fabric and cut the end of the thread to continue embroidering.

- Once your project has begun, you can secure the new stitches by passing them under several points adjacent to the back and continue embroidering.

Tips

- Start embroidering the model from the center of the canvas and go from corner to corner. For beginners and all other embroiderers, it is best to start in the middle and avoid a miscalculation.

- When embroidering, make sure your stitches are flat. If your thread begins to spiral, let go of the needle and let it hang. The thread unravels itself.

- Make sure your points all cross in the same direction.

- Keep your tension and your points equal

while embroidering your model.

- First, work the areas with markings and then fill the bottom.
- Work dark colors and then light colors.
- Sometimes you will embroider a few stitches for one area and then you will embroider in another area with the same color of thread. Moving from one area to another with the same thread may seem easier than stopping and picking up another thread, but if you keep the same color, the thread can be seen on the back of the canvas and make it visible at the location.
- Keep the same thread uncut only if the gap is small between the two areas and the thread is a light color.
- When you want to tie beads with cross-stitch, first work the cross-stitch diagonal, then tie the beads when you

work the back row. Make sure you use good quality beads because the plastic beads melt under the iron.

Here are some ideas:

- Put on crystal beads, crystals, charms, and small buttons. These can be interesting creative touches on a cross stitch pattern. 3D ornaments add interest to any embroidery and are available in many colors and styles.

Eyelet Stitch

Also known as the "star stitch", this stitch belongs to the counted stitches family. This is a very decorative stitch that can be used especially in traditional embroidery.

It usually consists of 8 branches in front that all meet in the center. The center then looks like an eye.

Eyelet is a simple stitch that you find a lot in

embroidery, but if it is poorly done it lacks beauty. It is embroidered from the outside towards the center and you pull your thread to make a hole in the center.

Necessary Tools:

- Punch Awl

The Technique

- Draw a circle on your fabric.
- Punch the fabric with the awl until the edges of your circle meet the tool.
- The hole will be the center of your eyelet stitch.
- Stitch a circle around the center using the straight stitch technique. Start as far or as close to the fabric as you want, depending on the size you want your eyelet stitch to be. Your stitched circle does not need to be perfect as it will be hidden by the branches of the eyelet stitch later.

- When you are done with your circle, pull the needle out from the center hole.
- Pick a stitch out of the circle and start creating your first branch by taking the needle back down in the hole and piercing the fabric right on the circle stitch you picked from the bottom.
- We are using the circle you stitched as a guideline.
- When you piece the fabric from the bottom, don't pull it all the way out.
- While your needle is still in the fabric, take the thread and bring it behind the needle to the opposite side.
- Pull your needle out.
- You should have your first branch now.
- Push the needle through the hole and pierce the fabric right next to your first branch.

- Bring the thread behind the needle and pull your needle out to create your second branch.

- Continue doing this until your circle is covered in branches and you can no longer see the stitched circle.

- To finish it off, flip the fabric to the wrong side, and pick the thread of a couple of the branches without the needle going through the fabric.

- Create a loop and bring your needle and thread through the loop to secure the stitch.

Rice Stitch

This stitch is obtained by alternately knitting a stitch and a reverse stitch on the same row, then thwarting the stitches on the next row. The number of stitches must be a multiple of 2.

It can sometimes be scary, but it will become

very easy if we stay focused on the work and the finished product is very beautiful.

The Technique

- This technique is best done on knitted fabric.

- Start by putting the needle through the bottom of the spot you want your design to start from.

- It is very important to note that the rice stitch is always worked on a base of even stitches. If you have an odd number of stitches, the stitch will not come outright. This is how a small mistake in your knitting can sometimes distort the whole project.

- Make your first stitch up towards the right side to start.

- Bring the thread back to the starting point of the work so you can do the next stitch upside down.

- Do the next stitch upside down, like an "X", then bring the thread back by passing it between the two legs to knit the next stitch.
- Continue by alternating row 1 and row 2 along the length desired to make your stitch knit.

Here are some ideas:

- Rice stitch works like cross-stitch but on knitted fabrics.
- Try using this technique instead of the duplicate stitch when you want a more detailed design on your knitted project.

Chapter 2: Historical Mending

Rafoogari

Rafoogari is an old, dying Indian technique of stitching. It is the ability to repair precious materials such as silk and cashmere. Rafoogari is an old art form, in which holes are stuffed so artfully that the points at which the fabrics were mended together should not be noticeable.

The Technique

- Working with your extra fabric, cut a piece that covers the hole in your garment. Make sure the piece is larger than the hole by at least 1 cm on each side.

- Pin the piece to your fabric inside the garment, so that the edges of the piece are not seen on the outside of the garment. When you have the garment facing you, with the outside fabric facing you, you should be able to see the hole, but also see your extra fabric inside the hole. Now it's time to stitch.

- Check the garment's stitching pattern. Is it a very fine stitch, or are they wider stitches with more gaps in them? You will need to follow the same stitching pattern in the same stitching direction.

- Using that pattern, sew along the edges of the piece you've placed over the hole. Then sew over the hole and the extra fabric using a running stitch and following the direction and size of the stitches of the garment. When you are finished, the hole should be completely hidden and seem to disappear into the fabric.

- You can do this with a sewing machine so that it goes quicker, or you can do it by hand in a more traditional way. Either way, go slowly, check your fabric often, and make sure your stitches are not standing out too much.

While it is a beautiful form of art on its own, people don't want to mention that they are wearing old pieces of fabric mended together. In cultures like the Indian culture, it might even be considered shameful; therefore, people no longer use this mending technique as much as they used to. Because of how hard it is to master, the low demand, and how much work it requires, Rafoogari has been slowly disappearing. In modern times, textile artists highlight the holes or space between the fabrics with colorful threads and plant fibers to try to bring the dying art form back to life. Working constructively with weaknesses creates a new way of performing this technique.

Sashiko

When translated from Japanese, sashiko means "small seams". The sashiko technique is sewn on the front of the fabric with visible stitches that are the size of a grain of rice. It uses a thick white thread on an indigo fabric made of vegetable fibers (flax, hemp, glycine). Cotton usage appeared more recently, and its use has become more common at the end of the 19th century.

Recently, Sashiko has become a very decorative embroidery technique used throughout the house: curtains, bags, clothes, tablecloths, etc. It's also used to strengthen the clothes of judo, kendo.

Followers of the traditional sashiko will do it on a more or less thick cotton cloth (kimono cloth) with a specific white thread. But it can be made on any fabric you choose, including cotton, linen, silk, wool, or on one with more thicknesses.

The Technique

- Specific cotton yarns are used in 1 or more strands but also pearl cotton, embroidery cotton, silk thread, mixed thread, metal, etc. can be used.

- Stitch on the front of the fabric, about 5 to 8 stitches per inch (= 2.5 cm). For example, quilting 8 to 12 stitches per inch, made without counting the frame or the border of the fabric.

- Needle, stitch length, and thread thickness needs to be adapted to the work according to thickness and type of work you are looking for.

To patch a hole or rip in your jeans, you can use the Sashiko technique to make it decorative. You will need spare fabric, the garment that needs to be repaired, and thread of a different color from your garment. The thread has to be a different color because it's not meant to blend in. Sashiko should stand out.

- First, find a fabric to use as a backing for the hole. It can be colorful, or the same color as the garment you're repairing.

- Pin the fabric to the jeans on the inside of the jeans leg. Remember to be careful while pinning and sewing. You don't want to accidentally sew your jeans closed. So, make sure that your pins are only connecting your spare fabric to the side of the jeans you want to sew.

- Choose a pattern you would like to sew onto the jeans. A really simple pattern is to use a wide-spacing running stitch in one direction, or both directions. You can also choose a pattern like a cross, boxes, waves, etc.

- Once you have your pattern, it's time to sew. Using your different colored thread, sew your pattern, starting from above your patch and continuing to below your patch. Once you are finished, tie off your thread and cut it.

Now you have a pair of beautifully decorated and patched jeans. This method can be used on a variety of fabrics and for a variety of reasons. It's mostly decorative, but it can easily be used for mending.

Most often, today, sashiko is made on a single layer of fabric. It can also sometimes be associated with patchwork.

It can be done on two or more layers by adapting the length of the stitches according to the thickness of the work:

2 layers of fabric (the 2nd being the lining)

1 layer of fabric + 1 layer of fleece: choose a fleece with little bulk: cotton or polyester, old towels or wool can do the trick! Beware of polyester fleeces whose fibers may come out with the embroidery (choose a dark colored fleece if the top fabric is dark). The lining is added later.

1 thickness of fabric + 1 thickness of fleece or other + 1 thickness of fabric (lining)

In principle, sashiko is not a reversible

embroidery technique. So, you must be careful when attempting it. The changes of direction will be concealed in the thickness of the work if you can hide it well. Sometimes, the threads are grouped and knotted in the corners of the garment to give it a smoother appearance.

Chapter 3: How to Darn

The times have changed, but it remains useful to know how to handle thread and needle. Here is a complete guide to the repair of clothing help you fix everything you need from sweaters and socks to jeans and pillows.

Helpful Tips for Darning for Beginners

The sewing box

- No need for a huge sewing box: the basic materials will fit in a shoebox or in a cookie tin perfectly.

- Pin the sewing and darning needles of different sizes into a pincushion or a piece of soap (the soap will help them slip more easily into thick, stiff fabrics). A magnet can also serve as a pincushion and will allow you to quickly pick up scattered needles.

- The pins and safety pins can be stored in a small box of matches.

- In addition, you will need sewing and darning thread in various colors, and possibly solid thread for thicker fabrics.

- Complete your box with a thimble, a darning ball, a quick-pick and scissors. A needle threader will also be useful.

- Over time, many buttons will accumulate in your box. To see more clearly, put together those that have the same color. As for the spare buttons, keep them in transparent bags, with a label indicating the name of the corresponding garment.

Buttons and boutonnieres

- Buttons can come loose or fall; it happens. Before losing it, at the risk of not finding a substitute, it is better to take the time to sew it securely.

- To avoid damaging the fabric by

disassembling the button, slide a comb between the fabric and the button. Then remove the remnants of the thread;

- Rub the thread with candle wax to stabilize it;
- Sew the four-hole button stitch, preferably crosswise with two threads. So, if one of them breaks, the button stays in place;
- To prevent the fabric of the button band from tearing, especially on the coats, sew another small button on the wrong side.
- Close a buttonhole that is distended or too big by stitching it upside down: make a few points from the outside to the center, so that the button just goes through. Stop the end with the thread.

Quick troubleshooting

- For stretch fabrics, sew the edges of the piece by hand.

- Holes in the wool should be hemmed, to prevent them from getting larger.
- To repair torn jeans, take a piece of other jeans that you no longer wear and sew it on the hole, inside.
- To easily thread a needle, spray some hairspray on the end of the thread.
- Transparent nail polish or the glue can certainly stop a mesh that pulls, like pantyhose, but remember that it cannot be repaired. It is therefore better to reserve this solution for emergencies. If you are not home when the problem occurs, apply moistened soap.
- Rub zippers with beeswax if they are hard to open and close. As for reused zippers, spray them with starch water, and then iron them: you can then sew them onto another garment.
- Replacing an elastic is a breeze: attach

the new elastic to the old one with a safety pin. Then remove the old one by gently pulling it: the new one will be put in place by itself.

- Threads will be stronger if you coat them with paraffin wax or wax.
- Do you have no thread of the right color on hand? Choose a darker tone than the original. Do not use a lighter thread.

Basic Darning

- Before you start sewing stitches, you need to knot one end of the thread. Then, prick the needle into the fabric by pushing it from the back of the fabric toward the spot you want to darn.
- You have to sew from right to left and leave a small regular space between each point. Take the needle out of A, replant it in B and take it out in C, and so on. With practice, you will learn to do 2-3 stitches

without taking the needle out of the fabric.

- Finish the seam with one or two back stitches.

- To finish the stitching, make a knot in the shape of an 8: make a small stitch, pass the thread inside the loop and pull. Do this 2 or 3 times to secure everything.

Darn a Hemline

- Fold the fabric after determining the width of the hem;

- Iron it, then secure it with pins;

- Sew the inside edge with the slipper stitch, from left to right, so that the hem does not get loose.

- Avoid stretching the thread too much.

- Then, iron the hem with a damp cloth between the iron and the fabric.

Pattern Darning

Things you will need:

- A very thick cardboard
- A long-blade cutter or a mini-saw or a sharp knife with teeth
- Wide elastic bands

The Technique

- Cut a hole in the center of your cardboard.
- Put your garment around the cardboard and stabilize it with the elastics.
- Start about 1 cm from the edge of the hole, making a stitch line in regular stitches.
- Keep going up until about 1 cm from the other side of the hole.
- When you reach the other side, go towards the direction of the hole and do the same thing.

- Continue until a square of stitches is formed around the hole.
- Stitch your way into the hole by continuing to stitch smaller squares.
- When your hole is covered loosely with the first stitch square, start stitching another square on top of the one you just stitched but create a pattern by going in the opposite direction so that the stitches create an "X".
- If your fabric is fragile or thin, do not pull too much on your thread; you will create the risk of tearing the fabric in another spot.

Mending the Holes in Your Favorite Sweater

There are multiple ways you can fix a hole in your sweater. If it is very small, just stitch it with some thread and needle by holding the fabric together. If the hole is as big as the width of your finger or bigger, use one of the techniques below.

Technique 1

Things you will need:

- Thread to match your sweater's thread
- A needle
- A darning mushroom, hard-boiled egg (cold), or lightbulb.
- Washable sewing marker, or disappearing ink sewing marker.

The Technique

- With the right side of the sweater facing you, place a darning mushroom, egg, or a lightbulb inside the sweater and under the hole. This will stabilize the hole for your sewing.
- Start by stitching around the hole to help prevent it from getting any larger. Place

the stitches about 1/4 inch away from the edge of the hole and use a running stitch or back stitch to go around the hole until you return to the starting point. Tie off the thread.

- To mend the hole, draw a square over it with the sewing marker. The square should be larger than the hole, with at least 1 cm of space above, below, and to the sides of the hole.

- Using a running stitch, fill in the square vertically. Make sure the stitched columns are close together and alternate the stitches. When you get to the hole, pass the thread over it and continue the running stitch past the hole.

- When you've completed the square with running stitches, go over it again, but this time horizontally. Weave the threads into the running stitch you made, moving back and forth. When you get to the hole, weave the thread between the stitches you made that passed over the hole. It should look like a basket weave when you are finished. Tie off the thread, pass the knot into the inside of the sweater, and cut the thread.

Technique 2

Things you will need:

- A couple of pieces of paper
- Scissors
- Fusible fabric
- An iron

The Technique

- Draw the desired shapes on the paper.
- Cut out the shapes.
- Turn the shapes over and place them on the lapel of the fabric (fusible side).
- Draw the outline with a pen.

- Cut out the fusible fabrics.
- Place the fusible parts on the area to be repaired and fix them on the iron (maximum temperature and pressure).

Darning a Sock

Few people today really know how to darn socks even though it is not that complicated. Instead of throwing your socks out, you can choose to darn them and keep using them. So, what to do when one of your socks is punctured?

The Technique

- Choose the right thread! Choose a thread. You must choose one whose color and thickness are as close as possible to those of your perforated sock.

You can also choose a dark thread for horizontal seams and a lighter color for vertical seams. If you have a sock of dark color, you can use white thread to see more clearly when you stitch and vice versa.

The thread you choose does not have to be the same color as the sock (unless you're a foot model, not many people will look at the seams of your socks).

- Thread the thread into the needle. Do it twice if the sock is thicker.
- Tie a knot at the end of the thread to fit the needle. Then start sewing the inside of the sock, so that the knot is not seen from the outside.
- Put a darning egg in the sock.
- If you do not have a darning egg or do not want to buy one, you can use a small round object instead, such as a tennis ball or a light bulb. You can also use your hand and slip it into the sock, as if it were a foot. However, this last option will make the task more difficult.
- Stitch the hole shut.

When the sock has thinned out

- Take the sock.

- Cut out the little threads that protrude from your sock. Using scissors, cut the sock so that the hole is more visible and easier to sew. Be careful not to enlarge the hole as well.

- Push the needle at one end of the hole. Then pass it on the other side of the hole, so that both ends are glued together. This is called a straight stitch, which is the most basic of the stitches.

- All you have to do is put your needle through the hole several times, so that the ends of the hole are connected to each other by the thread.

- You can also make a few stitches above the hole to reinforce the seam so that the hole does not reappear later.

- Repeat this operation. Continue until the

hole is completely sewn and covered with thread.

- You can now make points perpendicular to those you have just done (optional). This will further enhance the stitching you just created. For this, simply move your needle over the parallel points.

Tips!

- Try to stitch your sock before the hole is too big. Remember the adage: "prevention is better than cure"! If you darn your sock quickly, it will take less time and effort than if you wait too long.

- Be careful not to hurt yourself with the needle by threading or sewing. Wear a thimble if you are afraid of hurting yourself.

5 Darning Tools

Darning Egg

A darning egg. The haberdashery egg is made of wood but, failing that, one can take a chicken egg, hard-boiled preferably to avoid accidents.

How to use it?

- The principle is to replace the worn part by weaving crossed threads.
- Place the egg in the sock under the darning area and hold the egg and sock together in your left hand.
- Thread 1 to 4 strands of darning wool together in the needle (4 if it is a big hole in a big sock, 1 only if you just have to reinforce a beginning of wear). Do not tie knots.
- Begin 0.5 cm in width and height of the worn part.
- Make a row of straight stitches from 1 to 2 mm thick, from right to left.
- Turn the work half a turn to make a

second row of staggered dots, 1 to 2 mm from the first.

Darning Mushroom

The darling mushroom is a first cousin of the darning egg. It belongs to the big family of sewing objects. It is usually composed of a half ball flattened and a handle, which, for the mushroom, serves as a foot!

It has the same use as his cousins: put it in the damaged garment and place it at the level of the hole, in order to mend it. The cap of the mushroom makes it possible to maintain the tensioned fabric in order to facilitate the recovery or the staking of the perforated part. It offers a larger area for a wider recovery.

The wood used is very often a hardwood like oak or boxwood, which takes a nice texture over time. Some are left natural, and some are painted. They come in various sizes.

Tape measure

The tape measure is a must when talking about

sewing equipment. It allows you to take measurements easily and accurately. Whether it is to take your measurements, check the width of fabric, or measure the length of fabric you need for your project, it is simply essential.

Marker pen

They are soluble with water. They are used to mark the fabric before making cuts or stitches to create the perfect end result.

Tailor's scissors

These are big scissors (at least 20 cm long) intended to cut fabric and nothing but fabric!

The tailor's scissors are valuable and become dull if they are not used wisely. So, hide them, put a padlock on them, and threaten whoever approaches them. If they are used on anything other than fabric, they will be ruined.

Chapter 4: Patching Denim

Raw denim (without spandex) is a very stiff material especially if you are a follower of the skinny jean trend. Friction caused by walking tends to have an abrasive effect especially if your jeans are too wide or too big. You will quickly have holes in the hems, ankles, and buttocks, especially if you walk a lot in your day to go to work for example. On the other hand, if it is too small, the seams will have the annoying habit of letting go and ripping, especially around the thighs.

In short, if you want to keep your jeans for a long time, beyond choosing quality materials, you must be careful to take it to the right size with a cut adapted to your body type. The adjustment of the hems is also important because it allows you to stretch your legs and avoid the multiple folds that will rub against each other. This is all because fixing a hole in your jeans is not as easy as just stitching them back up. They will not look exactly the same as before.

Thankfully, there are techniques you can follow that will allow you to fix the hole in your denim clothes without cutting them into shorts. Let's look at a couple of the solutions below.

Fixing the Crotch

The crotch of a jean undergoes all kinds of wear: it is stretched, rubs against the thighs, and the seam can rip at the worst possible time. The crotch is the part that is most likely to crack or tear and create large or small holes. Instead of giving up and tossing damaged jeans, you can use various methods to repair them. A small tear can be sewn while for a larger hole, you will need a piece of cloth.

- Cut the threads that hang around the damaged part. You can repair small holes without extra fabric, simply by sewing the edges of the hole or torn part together. Before doing so, take scissors and cut the strings protruding from the edges of the hole so that they are clear. Otherwise, the strings will hinder you when you sew. When cutting the strings, be careful not to enlarge the hole.

- Cut only the threads that protrude, not the fabric itself.
- Thread a needle and knot the thread correctly. If you tie the opposite end of the thread, it will remain anchored in the fabric when you start sewing. It can be annoying to have to thread the needle constantly, so be sure to catch the thread.
- Sew the edges of the hole to prevent them from fraying even more. Reinforce the edges of the damaged part by "closing" them with small looping dots. Be careful not to make these dots so close to the edges that the thread simply damages more of the jean's fabric. This step is

optional, but it can help prevent the fabric around the hole from fraying and make your repair more resistant.

- The scallop and buttonhole stitch are good choices for this step.
- Sew the hole in the garment to close it. Flatten the fabric or hold it so that the hole in the jeans is completely closed. Make a vertical seam over the hole to close it. You may need to iron several times for the repair to be resistant. Begin the dots about 1 cm from one of the edges of the hole. Finish them about 1 cm from the other edge of the hole.
- As you pass the other side of the hole, make points smaller and smaller.
- Pull the thread to tighten it, knot it and cut off the end so that nothing sticks out
- These points should be at least 1 cm away from those you have sewn to reinforce

the edges of the hole.

- You can also do this at the sewing machine, but if the hole is very small, it can be just as easy to repair by hand.

Adding Fabric to the Crotch

- Cut the thread protruding around the hole. Using a piece of fabric is ideal if you do not feel like you are able to sew or simply want to do a quick repair. This might be a good solution for a work jean whose utility is more important than appearance.

- Cut out a piece of fabric the right size. Flip the jeans over and take a piece of fabric over old jeans or use any other piece of fabric that you want to sew on the hole. Make sure there is plenty of fabric well around the torn part so that you can apply glue.

- Put some textile glue on the piece. Follow

the specific instructions on the bottle. In general, apply the glue to the edges of the fabric. Be careful not to put glue on the part of the fabric that will be seen on the outside of the jeans. Place the fabric on the hole, press it down and hold it in place.

- The drying time depends on the glue used, but it should not be longer than a few hours.

Use a fusible fabric

- Prepare the hole to repair. A fusible fabric is a simple solution if you do not want to sew it on. As with all other methods, first cut the threads so that the edges of the fabric are clean then turn the jeans and prepare the fabric that you will stick with the iron. Measure the hole with a measuring tape and cut the fabric to the correct size, making sure it is at least 1 cm wider around the hole.

- You can measure the fabric by eye, but with a tape measure, you are less likely to deceive yourself and waste the product by cutting a piece too small.

- If you cut rounded corners, the fabric will be less likely to come off.

- Place the fabric on the outside of the hole. If you stick it on the wrong side, the two sides of the pants could merge. If this happens, the leg of your jeans might remain closed and you won't be able to put your legs through.

- Iron the fabric on. Once your iron is hot, put the fabric on the hole and iron it. The time you must keep the iron on the fabric depends on each type of fusible fabric, so read the instructions and stick to them. In general, do not leave the iron in place for more than thirty to sixty seconds.

- Once the fabric glue is dry, your jeans will be ready.

Sewing a Piece of Fabric to Repair a Larger Hole

- Find a piece of suitable fabric. Sewing a piece of fabric is the most effective way to repair a big hole in the crotch, but also the one that requires the most work. You must have basic skills in hand sewing, but when you're done, the result should be cleaner and more resistant than a bonded or heat-sealed fabric. Start by finding a piece that fits the hole in your jeans.

- If you put the fabric on the back of the pants, choose a color as close as possible to that of your jeans so that the repair is not seen too much.

- If you want to have fun or do something light, you can let your creativity run wild when you choose the fabric.

- Make sure the fabric is not thicker than

your jeans. If it is not flexible enough to follow your movements, the fabric will tear.

- Cut out a piece of fabric that is at least 2.5 cm larger than the hole. If you cut the fabric parallel to the warp or weft, the edges are more likely to fray.
- Lay the jeans flat and pin the fabric on it. Make sure the fabric is not wrinkled or taut; otherwise the extra fabric will be taut or will form a lump. Unless you want to patch the damaged part with colorful or very showy fabric, slip the fabric inside the jeans to keep it in place.

Hemming Jeans

It's almost impossible to find jeans at the right leg length when you buy them in stores. If you have found a pair that suits you but is too long, you can bring it to a tailor or make a hem yourself. You can keep the original hem, or you can make a new one. Remember that it can be difficult to work with jeans, but by following a few simple methods, you can ensure a successful result.

Keep the original hem

- Decide on the location of the hem. Try the jeans and decide where you want to put the hem. In general, jeans should be between 2 and 3 cm above the ground. This will prevent you from stumbling and having pants that look too small. Feel free to change the length of the legs to suit your personal preferences.

- Fold down. Make a crease where you want to see the hem. Press the fold so that it is flat and check it to see if you have folded it properly. Once you have done it on one side, measure it just under the original hem and use this measurement to create a similar fold on the other leg.

- Keep it in place. Put needles all around the leg of the pants to hold it in place. Make sure that the seams are aligned on the same leg and aligned with each other.

- Sew the hem. Sew stitches all around the leg of the pants just below the points of the original hem. You can do it with a sewing machine or by hand. Now you have to sew the back of your leg before folding it in later. This will allow you to pull out the hem later if you are growing up or want the pants to be longer.

- Unfold the hem. Push the excess fabric into the leg of the trousers by folding the original hem down so that the outer side can be seen. This should leave a small loop of fabric along the edge of the jeans inside the leg. Try your jeans to make sure it's the right length.

- If you do not think that you will ever want to have longer pants, you can also cut the end of the fabric. Cut the excess fabric about 2 cm from the hem you just made.

- Iron the jeans. Use an iron to flatten the hem that you have created along the edge. This will flatten the fabric loop inside while getting pants to the right length without any sign of changes.

Create a new hem

- Make a mark at the location of the hem. The best way to do this is to put on your pants (or ask someone to wear it) and bend your lower leg until you get the length you like. Then use a piece of chalk to mark where you want to see the hem.

- Measure and mark two more lines. Measure 1 cm from the hemline and draw a line above parallel to the first. Then measure another 1 cm and make a mark below the original line and draw a new line parallel to the first.

- You should now have three lines. They will serve as a guide to sew the hem.
- Cut along the bottom line. Cut the bottom of the pants and the old hem. To do this, simply cut a straight line along the bottom line that you have drawn. Discard the fabric you just cut.
- Fold the new hem from below. Then, fold it along the middle line to make the new hem. You should also put needles to hold it in place while you sew it. Make sure the hem is in place all the way around before you start sewing.
- Sew the hem you just folded. Take gold thread for your choice of jeans or yarn and sew all around the area you have just held with the needles. Use a straight stitch and try to keep it as even as possible.
- Take out the needles as you go.

- After sewing the two hems, your jeans are ready to wear!

How to make DIY Ripped jeans

- Buying already torn jeans can be expensive. But, good news! It's easy to tear up yours. By following the right steps, with the right material and patience, you can quickly and easily rip your jeans.

- Choose jeans that fit you well. You can rip any jeans and get the same result, but do not feel obliged to rip one that you already have since you can find other cheap ones in thrift stores.

- Using jeans that have already been worn a bit will give better results than brand new jeans, but do not stop if you want to buy a new one for this project.

- Washed light-colored jeans are usually prettier when torn, as their color gives them a more worn look. The darker faded jeans seem too freshly dyed to be torn and will not be as "realistic".

- Gather your materials. All you need to tear your jeans are jeans and a sharp object. However, depending on the style you want, you will probably need to use a cutting tool.

- If you want to make holes, use scissors, a razor, or a sharp knife. The cutters also work.

- To create a frayed look, use sandpaper, cheese grater, or pumice.

- Choose a place to tear. Spread your jeans on a table and use a pencil to mark the places you want to rip. Use a ruler to mark the exact length you want. Keep in mind the last cut as well as the length, and the width of the holes.

- Generally, most people only tear at the

knees, although it is possible to tear the lower legs of the jeans.

- Just aim a little higher than your knee so that the tear does not become too big when you walk. Whenever your knee bends, it will take in the hole and tear it further.

- Do not tear too high.

- Spread the jeans on a flat surface. Slip a small piece of wood into the jeans' legs as you relax, so that you do not change the front and back of the jeans.

If not, you can even use cardboard, an old book, a stack of magazines, or anything else you can cut without worry. Do not do it on the kitchen table if you use a very sharp knife.

- Start fraying the jeans with the sandpaper. Before you start cutting, use sandpaper or iron straw to start scrubbing and thinning the place you want to tear. This will help you soften the fibers of the jeans and make it easier to tear.

- Use a lot of different tools; alternate between sandpaper, iron straw, and pumice stone. It may take a little while depending on the thickness of your jeans.

- If you prefer to just cut jeans, go for it. You do not have to weaken it unless you want it to look frayed.

- Soften the fibers further to make holes. If you want frayed areas and threadlike bands, use your scissors or knife to pull the area you have weakened with sandpaper. This will soften the fibers, letting a little skin appear when you wear jeans. Pull the white threads that come out of the jeans to exaggerate the look.

- Add holes with the knife or scissors. Take your scissors and cut a small piece of the relaxed area. Cut a little bit. You can still enlarge it, but you risk ruining your jeans and make it difficult if the hole is too big. Aim for a tear no larger than one centimeter.

- Make the tear in the direction of the width, not from bottom to top. It will look more natural.

- Use your hands to tear the jeans further. The tearing will pull on the fibers and give them the appearance of a real hole. Pull the strings out, as if they were real tears.

- Avoid cutting the hole too much, as this will give it very clean and unnatural edges.

- Otherwise, you can just make a small hole and let it grow as you wear your jeans. It will look more natural that way.

- Reinforce your jeans if you want. To

prevent the holes from getting larger, reinforce them by sewing around their perimeter. Use white or blue thread to sew around the tear, by hand, or machine.

- Go out with your cool jeans!

Advice

- Washing the jeans right after tearing them will make the fibers soften more and give an even more faded look.

- Avoid adding tears near the seams as they may start to distort.

- For an even more worn look, you can add bleach stains.

- For precise tears, use a sewing needle to pull the stitches one by one.

- If you are a man, avoid tearing too high, otherwise, we will see your underwear. For women, do the same by not exposing too much skin near your underwear.

How to make DIY Frayed jeans

While some have found their happiness in the shop, others have instead chosen the economic option of DIY by manufacturing their frayed hem on old jeans. It's a technique that's easy to master, provided you do it right. Here's a very simple little tutorial on how to make a frayed hem without screwing up your jeans.

- Take your tape measure and start by accurately measuring the length at which you want to place the hem.
- Pin where you want the hem to finish and fraying to start.
- Whatever you do, do not forget that the operation will shorten the length of the jeans a little and multiple machine washes will add to it.
- Once you are done pinning, use your scissors to cut the fabric as straight as possible.

- Then use your tweezers to pull some threads and fray your jeans.

- To complete the whole, perfect the operation, take some sandpaper and extract some more thread from the jeans.

- That's it, it's over, and you can put on your jeans! Obviously, the technique is also valid for any other piece of the same style such as a dress, shorts or denim skirt.

Why should you NOT wash your jeans?

The mistake that most people make is to think of jeans as regular pants. Jeans are not like a cotton chino that you can machine wash as often as you want. Would you wash your suit pants in a machine? Well, jeans have their specificities that must be respected, especially when they are raw jeans of good quality. Incidentally, if you have ecological beliefs, know that if the clothing lovers only wear raw jeans, it's because the canvas was not treated with chemicals like faded jeans. If your jeans are ripped, torn or worn out too much, washing them before mending them will only cause the damage to get worse. It is best to first fix the damage in your jeans and then wash it, if you must.

However, whatever the quality of your jeans, you must avoid washing it too often. And if you value your quality jeans, you should try hand washing them rather than a washing machine cycle.

Adding Frills to Your Jeans

You can use different styles of fabric to patch your jeans or to just add more decoration to them. One easy way to do this is to incorporate doilies and store-bought frills into your jeans. Using doilies to patch your jeans will create a really interesting pattern in the holes. You'll still see some skin through the hole, but you'll also have a lovely bohemian look to your jeans.

The Technique

To add doilies to your jeans, you'll need some thread that matches your jeans color, and a doily that looks nice and has already been washed. If you need to cut your doily, make sure that you hem the cut ends, so it doesn't unravel.

- Place the doily behind the hole in your jeans. Pin it to the jeans carefully to ensure you're not closing the jeans.

- Once everything is pinned, use a basic running-stitch to stitch the doily around the hole in your jeans, about 1.5 cm out from the hole itself.

- Do a second row at 1 cm away from the hole, to make sure that the doily is secure and won't move after being washed.

- Tie off the thread and cut it, hiding the ends inside the jeans.

To add doilies to the outside of your jeans, like on the sides or at the pockets, you can use washable fabric glue to add the doily to the fabric. You can follow these same techniques for adding frills, lace, or crochet to your jeans.

How to mend and style thrift store finds

Buying from thrift stores efficiently takes time, but you can find beautiful, functional items for your home and wardrobe without breaking the bank. In addition, when you shop at charity bargain stores, you can support worthy organizations that help your less fortunate neighbors.

To develop a good second-hand store strategy, understand the differences between the different types of stores that sell used goods. For example, you will not find many high-end brands in standard thrift stores, but mail-order stores often sell branded clothing in good condition. What you can do is fix and style the old clothes you find in a thrift store to give them a new life and a different look.

You can stitch small tears and add different fabrics to worn-out clothes. If you find an item that you really like, but needs some modifications or damage repair, consider repairing or resizing the item to suit you. You save so much money by buying second-hand clothes that you can still pay for small repairs. The rapidly growing second-hand fashion market remains an economic, ecological and eco-responsible solution for extending the life of a garment. This craze is explained by an awareness of the wastage of clothing. To stock up, there are of course the charity shops you can find amazing things for a very cheap price. Consider:

- Adding sequins or lace to your finds
- Shorten long skirts or dresses and throw on a belt to freshen them up
- Switch the old buttons on cardigans or jackets with new buttons
- Replace the zipper on pants with new

zippers

Tips!

- Make sure the piece is still in good condition

If it is really damaged, you can always ask for an additional discount and repair it yourself at home. However, from experience, if the piece is too damaged or old, it is not worth it.

- Evaluate price and quality

What I mean is that you do not get too excited about the price. Even if it's really cheap, it's not necessarily worth it and the opposite is true! It's not because it's a bit more expensive than it's worth. We must evaluate the piece, its quality, the number of times you wear it, etc. too.

It is a mandatory step to not be fooled by the low prices of thrift stores. The garment can be damaged, the fabric too old and fragile, and so on. So feel free to touch the material, read the composition labels by focusing on the noble materials (cotton, silk...), and make an inventory of the garment in its entirety to ensure that there is no stain or no hitch.

I also advise you to check the tags which can be a good indicator with regards to the quality and durability of the garment. Keep in mind that the clothing has already lived and has been worn, so a piece of a low-end brand is not necessarily a good deal. In case of an unknown brand or lack of brand label, look at the seams and finishes. But of course, the decision is up to you!

- Go early to get the best stuff

This may seem obvious, but to put all our chances on our side, it is better to go early. You should know that most thrift shops add to their stores every day, so the best deals of the day go first. In the end, it's a bit like during sales. So, we get up early (and in a good mood) to maximize its chances of finding the rare pearl.

Thrifty requires a lot of patience. When entering a thrift store, keep in mind that it is not Zara,

Mango, or any other brand of ready-to-wear, and that the brands, when there are there, are not always organized. You have no choice but to search again and again. Nevertheless, imagine the satisfaction of finding a beautiful piece that was there, buried in a tray among so many other vintage clothes and that no one has seen.

- Be open-minded to change

I know, sometimes we would like to find THE perfect outfit that makes us dream for weeks, to no avail. This can be discouraging, but it is necessary to persevere and not be blinded by this coveted garment. Because by having a precise idea of the desired piece, you end up being disappointed and no longer see the other pieces that have as much potential, if not more.

- Consider every aspect

There are two questions to ask yourself when you are about to make a purchase in a thrift store, which I think is essential: "Can I imagine this piece in a current outfit?" And "Do I really like this piece?". Admittedly, we do not necessarily go into a second-hand shop to add a vintage touch to a current outfit: some also go because it's a good way to create a very unique, personal style. Nevertheless, I observe that most people (me included) make mixes between modern and retro. But to be able to mix a vintage piece and not regret its purchase, we must be able to transpose it to our time and especially, do not force yourself to like a piece under the pretext that "it's vintage and cheap".

Chapter 5: 10 Sewing Tips!

Below are some tips about sewing both by hand and sewing machine to give you a little bit more information and insight into the sewing world. By remembering and practicing these tips, you will be able to approach any sewing project with confidence. Eventually, you will learn things from your own projects and will have your own tips to share with people.

If you are worried about not doing things the correct way, good news! There are plenty of little tips for sewing right.

Tip 1: Do not look at the needle

Do not fix your eyes on your needle. Take a wider look and see what's around the needle instead. Focus on the fabric and observe how it stands and behaves throughout the seam.

Tip 2: Define your creative project

Always remember to take the time to choose your project carefully. It can be a response to a need, or just a small pleasure to create. In any case, take note of the material you will need and select your fabric according to your project (the yardage is very often indicated). Try to have a clear idea of what you want to accomplish before you start. This way, you will make sure to ace all of your projects by practice.

Tip 3: Work on things you know you will like

If necessary, download or buy a pattern that you cut or copy. The internet is full of free and paid examples, so take the time to choose your favorites! The more you like your project, the better you will be able to focus on it.

Tip 4: Take your time

When you start, you must avoid rushing too much. Take the time to sew your stitches one by one, readjusting if necessary. You will find it to be easier for you to sew right than if you sew at a higher speed like the professionals. You will adjust your speed eventually. For now, take it slow.

Tip 5: Draw a line with chalk

You can also draw your chalk line in advance.

Thus, at the time of sewing, you will only have to follow the line and be able to sew right without too much difficulty.

Tip 6: Train yourself

Before actually sewing your project, familiarize yourself with your sewing machine by sewing straight and parallel lines on a piece of fabric, such as a piece of cloth or clothing. Test different stitches and vary the tension and the length of the stitches to better understand your machine.

If you are sewing by hand, practice doing regular stitches that will inevitably be more aesthetic on a piece of trial fabric before you move onto the costly fabrics.

Tip 7: Prepare your fabric

Whether for clothing or accessories, you will need to wash and prepare your fabric! That means you will also need to iron it so that it is wrinkle-free and ready to work on. Preparing the fabric will also keep the bad surprises away. You will know how the fabric washes, if it shrinks, or loses color before sewing and putting effort on it.

Tip 8: Using a magnetic stitching guide

There are magnetic sewing guides to block your fabric. You can use these instead of pinning the fabric down or using wood hoops. Find these magnetic guides online or at your local craft store to give them a try. You never know which one of these techniques you will like better.

Tip 9: Move your needle

If you are learning to use the sewing machine, move your needle to the left if you want a seam allowance of 1cm. Move it until the distance between the right edge of the crowbar and your needle is 1 cm and then place the edge of your fabric along the right edge of the crowbar. Thus, you will sew a seam margin of 1cm.

Tip 10: Get started!

You have fallen for a fabric, you have your project in mind, and all your equipment ready. Now is the time to start! Do not postpone your projects. If you don't start when you are super excited about it, you will probably keep postponing it. With the help of this book and the internet, you can learn and master any stitching technique.

Conclusion

For millennia, knowing how to sew has been considered a plus in many societies. Thus, more and more people are talking about sewing, and not just clothing. Moreover, we notice today that a large number of people want to learn how to sew. If you are wondering why sewing is becoming a common hobby again these days, we have some answers below.

Because sewing is an activity that brings people together

To strengthen family ties or strengthen bonds with friends, sewing is a fun activity everyone can do together. Imagine having a friend who knows how to sew like you. When you talk, you can talk about your latest creations. She is impressed by what you have done, and you are impressed by what she did. Everyone asks the other to tell them how to do certain things. This will result in hours of passionate discussion where you will be able to join the conversation.

Children can both learn a crucial life skill while having fun with you when you are teaching them how to sew. Sewing can also be a way to get closer to yourself; to discover you in another aspect.

Because learning how to sew is easy

Learning sewing today is easy. All you need is a needle, some thread, maybe a sewing machine for beginners and some tools, and you're ready. There are a lot of courses, tutorials, tips, and free patterns on the internet that can be used to learn quickly and easily. Thus, with the prospect of learning easily, sewing becomes much more attractive and conceivable. But you have to know how to be patient and willing to practice before managing to sew the gown of your dreams.

Because knowing how to sew saves money

Learning to sew saves money. If for example a shirt loses a button, it can be replaced quickly, without spending too much money on a new outfit or a seamstress or tailor. You can also patch a garment quickly and wear it. But knowing how to sew does not only make it possible to patch, but also to sew brand new things from simple fabrics.

You can make pillowcases, wallets, tea towels, bags, and even dresses for yourself. It will take time, but with practice, the speed comes, and we spend less money sewing than for a purchase in a store or shop.

Because you deserve to wear clothes that fit you perfectly

When you get comfortable in your sewing, you can create amazing things that fit you like a glove. No need to spend a ton of money on designer clothing due to their tailored fit.

If you see a high fashionable garment that you like, but you cannot afford to buy, you can choose your own fabric and sew the model of your choice. You can also create custom clothing that looks and reflects your personality. To wear tailor-made clothing and stand out without spending a fortune, learn sewing even if it's online. It's the best option, not to say it's the only one, for keeping up your wardrobe.

References

9 Sewing Skills You Gotta Nail to Become a Total Master. (2019, July 11).

Retrieved from https://www.mybluprint.com/article/wanna-be-a-sewing-master-first-you-gotta-nail-these-9-skills

DH News Service. (2013, April 13). Rafoogari: Art of darning. Retrieved from https://www.deccanherald.com/content/325696/rafoogari-art-darning.html

Racklin, M. (2019, March 25). Instead of hiding rips and tears, the visible mending movement turns them into art.

Retrieved from https://www.vox.com/the-goods/2019/3/25/18274743/visible-mending-sashiko-mending-fast-fashion-movement

Repairing Jeans with Invisible Mending. (2018, April 10). Retrieved from https://closetcasepatterns.com/repairing-jeans-with-invisible-mending/

Sashiko Mending Is a Clothing Life Saver. (n.d.). Retrieved from https://www.diynetwork.com/made-and-remade/fix-it/repair-holes-in-pants-with-sashiko

WeAllSew. (2018, July 30). Basic Sewing Techniques for Beginners. Retrieved from https://weallsew.com/basic-sewing-techniques-for-beginners/

What is Rafoogari? (n.d.). Retrieved from https://craftatlas.co/crafts/rafoogari

CPSIA information can be obtained
at www.ICGtesting.com
Printed in the USA
LVHW111316230420
654315LV00003B/704

9 781951 035174